EVENT HORIZON

EVENT HORIZON

Or How My Business Career Got Sucked into the Black Hole
of the Radical Change in the Computer Industry

MICHAEL STOCKDELL

Event Horizon

Copyright © 2019 by Michael Stockdell. All rights reserved.

No part of this publication may be reproduced, stored in a retrieval system or transmitted in any way by any means, electronic, mechanical, photocopy, recording or otherwise without the prior permission of the author except as provided by USA copyright law.

The opinions expressed by the author are not necessarily those of URLink Print and Media.

1603 Capitol Ave., Suite 310 Cheyenne, Wyoming USA 82001
1-888-980-6523 | admin@urlinkpublishing.com

URLink Print and Media is committed to excellence in the publishing industry.

Book design copyright © 2019 by URLink Print and Media. All rights reserved.

Published in the United States of America

ISBN 978-1-64367-906-8 (Paperback)
ISBN 978-1-64367-905-1 (Digital)

30.09.19

Contents

Introduction: What This Book Is About? 7
Chapter 1: My Business Career Wanes 19
Chapter 2: The Peculiar Way I Relate To The World...................26
Chapter 3: The Insight Of A Lifetime..34
Chapter 4: Company Culture Becomes A Factor.......................46
Chapter 5: The Early Computer Industry 61
Chapter 6: IBM's Absolute Dominance Over The
 Computer Industry 72
Chapter 7: How IBM's Culture Influenced Its Market
 Dominance 88
Chapter 8: The IBM Image Comes In Conflict With
 The Changing Social Paradigm 99
Chapter 9: How IBM Was Vulnerable In Spite Of Its
 Marketing Clout 112
Chapter 10: I Search For The Deeper Implications Of
 IBM's Problems..129
Chapter 11: The New Social Paradigm Penetrates The
 Computer Industry 142
Chapter 12: The New Paradigm Takes Hold..............................158
Chapter 13: The New Paradigm Begins To Affect
 Business Data Processing...172
Chapter 14: A Summary Of The Technology Driving
 The Computer Industry..186
Chapter 15: How Ideology In The Computer Industry
 Led To Rejection Of My Ideas.................................193
Chapter 16: The Fear Of Technological Obsolescence
 Also Works Against Me 202

Chapter 17: My Lack Of Paper Qualifications And
　　　　　　Unconventional Marketing Methods Work
　　　　　　Against Me 211
Chapter 18: The Conclusion To My Business Career 223
Chapter 19: What Happened Next 230

INTRODUCTION

WHAT THIS BOOK IS ABOUT?

Why Event Horizon? Some of you who have an interest in astrophysics might recognize that term as describing the extremely bright edge of a black hole, that point beyond which matter is sucked into the black hole never to be seen again.

What does that have to do with anything in the computer industry? Well, the period of the late 1980s and early 1990s was a time when it first became apparent to me that the industry was going to change; that soon IBM would lose its iron grip on the industry. Everything in the entire industry would change and many IBM-related businesses would be sucked into the black hole of history. It hadn't happened yet but I knew it would and had deduced many of the consequences to the industry when it did.

Because I was thought of as an old-time systems analyst and because I was relaying the bad news about IBM, my business career also wound up getting sucked away.

oOo

Most books which purport to tell the history of computing start way back with the Jacquard loom or the difference engine, that is, with various devices and ideas that led to the modern digital computer. This is not that kind of book.

Instead, it is a history of the whole computer industry, software, hardware, firmware, peripherals, as seen through my eyes during the years I was involved in the industry. I will spend a little space discussing the time before and the time after this period, because there is no historical event that doesn't depend on the past. And the present is merely a prelude to the future. The book is a mix of memoir and criticism, with passages relating to my thirty-year career in the information systems business.

At different times in my career I worked on both the commercial applications and scientific sides of the industry. I managed a business systems group, was a higher education consultant, an executive with a startup parallel supercomputer company, and the inventor of Digital Equipment Corporation's consulting business. All with an undergraduate degree in English.

But always as an analyst, planner, and conceptualizer, and never as a hard-skilled technician – never a computer circuitry designer, or a developer of analog to digital computing applications or, for that matter, a business computer programmer.

In spite of this lack of "hard" technical skills, I learned a great deal over the years, from books and magazines and plain experience about the logic of computing as a business. In particular I learned that the computer industry obeys rules that are radically different from any other kind of commercial enterprise. Trying to treat it according to traditional rules alone often results in unpleasant surprises for stock analysts, business owners, and investors. On the other hand, to treat it like a *rara avis* that is so different from ordinary business that traditional rules don't apply at all is to expose the analyst to wishful thinking or naïve decision-making. A classic case of the latter built large was the Internet bubble around the turn of the millennium.

Now bubbles happen all the time. If you don't think so read Charles Mackey's *Extraordinary Popular Delusions and the Madness of Crowds*.

But the collapse of the Internet bubble of 2000-2001 was different from previous economic panics. It involved technologies that were not well understood. Many believed any clever new idea was going to be successful just because it involved a new way of doing business.

Yet if you had some understanding of what was really at stake you knew that nothing about the Internet boom made sense. Hell, I knew everything was going down the tubes months in advance of the exploding bubble.

I remember an incident where I saw on television an Indian guy (at the time Indians were considered the last word in technology) who said that all these Internet companies raising tens of millions of dollars on a wish and a prayer made all kinds of sense. I'm generally a mild-mannered guy but my face turned red and I yelled at the television set, "Fools", I said. As has happened so many times in my career, I was right when everybody else was wrong and the inevitable happened. As a consequence, many companies went broke and the entire economy was brought to its knees. Too bad I didn't have enough money to sell some of these companies short.

The Internet bubble differed from previous mass delusions in that in most cases people learned from their mistakes and Tulipomania was never repeated. In the computer industry history repeats itself over-and-over again, only on a much smaller scale. If a computer "platform" fails, it may take a whole bunch of other businesses along with it, many of whom you've never heard of. Sun Microsystems, once the leader in the engineering workstation business, wound up being swamped by Personal Computers and remains a shadow of its former self with only Java software remaining from the previously large business. When Sun went down, all the other workstation companies went down with it. As did most of the vendors that made compatible software and hardware applications.

There are many computer-related companies now, some quite well-known, some with absurdly high valuations that will eventually go the same way as Sun. There is an intrinsic risk in the technology industry and that is the likelihood of obsolescence. You have to guess right all the time.

If one looks deeply into the causes of the Internet fiasco. the peculiar personality of computer technicians, who seem to the world to be a particularly hard-minded bunch, has to be seen as a major factor. Many technicians have very poor social skills and seem to have little sense of the practical and every day. Building the product is everything, marketing it is incidental. Some seem to be and may actually suffer from borderline autism, able to concentrate on only one idea for days at a time with the outside world never impinging. They are truly wonderful in working with the concrete and objective. Properly directed they can create wonders.

Too often, however, they want to run their own businesses for which most have little capacity. In the 1980s and 1990s venture capitalists threw huge sums of money at them, believing that their technical capabilities and good ideas were enough, only to have poor management flush away the investment. This continues to happen today.

We never seem to learn from the past.

There are a few engineers and programmers who have good business sense or know they don't have it and hire it. The plethora of successful companies that have survived a while attests to that.

A good idea can make a person a fortune overnight even without wonderful social skills, because the image and usefulness of the product is often a different thing from any one personality. Who knows what Sergei Brin looks like? Yet he is half of the genius behind Google. You can always hire a good salesman or administrative manager.

The dominance of engineers and programmers in the industry is just the opposite of the way it was in the beginning. Salesmen ruled the roost. Technical people were hidden away in labs in Armonk, New York or around Route 128 near Boston or in Rochester, Minnesota. The more gregarious of the field systems engineers for, say, IBM, might wind up helping customers without seeming too unconventional. Every once in a while, you'd find one who looked good in a business suit and was articulate enough to make a stand-up presentation to a CEO of a giant company. These could be promoted to account (sales) manager. This was, however, almost never the case for those who started out as Customer Engineers (CEs), the title IBM gave to the men (back then, they were virtually all men) who fixed and installed the hardware.

This was a time when IBM (the International Business Machines Company) controlled 75% of the entire computer industry. IBM was so powerful that the Federal government required Big Blue to divest itself of the Service Bureau Corporation (its systems development arm) as a part of the settlement of an interminable antitrust suit in the 1960s and 1970s, This action had no noticeable effect on IBM's performance, however, because almost all computer systems were still being developed by internal computer departments. And it cleared the way for many applications software companies, whose products could not be run on any other vendor's machines and locked the customers into IBM technology. IBM's mastery of the industry continued, challenged but never approached, for nearly thirty years from the early fifties to the mid-1980s. It was still a power to be reckoned with, by far the largest and most profitable company in the industry for fifteen or twenty years more. Even today, IBM remains a very large business and is dominant in a couple of industry segments, the slowly dying mainframe business and super-high performance computing coupled with Artificial Intelligence, such as the Deep Blue computer that beat world chess champion Gary Kasparov.

And yet the underlying dynamics of the industry that nearly destroyed IBM were always there in plain sight even in the early days of computing. One example: software not hardware was always the driving force in the industry. It was IBM's OS platform and its slightly less sophisticated companion DOS (for medium-sized businesses) that gave it such dominance. Whenever a better technical platform challenged IBM, its technology was never able to compete with Big Blue's proprietary operating system and rich catalogue of software and third-party vendors.

There were exceptions, however. In the 1980s so-called minicomputers (really a way of building hardware systems not a description of the size of a machine), led by Digital Equipment Corporation, dominated academic, scientific, and engineering computing and were a force in so-called distributed business applications (more about this later). IBM was never able to compete in this space, largely because its systems were too expensive, did not upgrade easily, and did not communicate well with each other (an inevitable consequence of OS and the machines built around it).

This is little different from, say, Radio Shack's TRS-80 being unable to compete with the Apple II and its superior user experience.

oOo

This book is also about me as a denizen of the industry from the early days until the 1990s when I was driven out of it. I lost out because I had a boutique notion of the way software development firms should be organized and the industry wasn't ready for it. This was an era when generalists ruled and I was proposing highly specialized systems development. Some service companies were no more than body shops, where a company would contract for a specialized talent they couldn't hire on their own. Others saw enhanced profitability in outsourcing. In those instances where an individual could sell themselves as an expert on a particular application, they were usually expert in a particular piece of software or the way a particular application was customarily implemented. Or where an application or technical specialty was in short supply and they possessed it.

I believed I had a real opportunity to revolutionize the services industry given my understanding that IBM was beginning to lose its grip and many applications were due for replacement. The available technology was even then changing so fast that new applications were going to be designed in a very different way in the future. Computer power was going to be local and not remote, and many systems were going to be designed around immediate posting of results instead of being held in queue waiting for some batch process to be run. Payroll data would be gathered every day instead of once every couple of weeks. Customer orders would be processed as they were received not overnight. And so forth. All this would require a radical redesign of existing applications in ways IBM's technology was not structured to handle. Further, the IBM marketing structure was in direct conflict with the social and political changes of the sixties and seventies.

What I didn't realize was that my ideas and insights threatened the received wisdom in the industry. Further, I lacked the right personality and training to be a part of the new emerging social dynamic. I looked like a classic IBM-type manager, not an unreformed hippy. In an industry that was turning to turnkey applications I was always perceived as more of a big picture guy rather than a hands-on type, although I could tell you exactly what had gone wrong with a computer program and knew enough about technology that I could strategize with the best of them. I was considered not very technical even though I could design an application down to the subroutine, I never laid down a line of code in my entire career. And never wanted to. I had too many projects in mind for that.

The time I am referring to was the late 1980s and early 1990s. I began my career doing systems studies in the Department of Agriculture in the late 1960s. Then, after working at A.H.Robins Company in Richmond, VA. for a couple of years, I developed a list of objectives for all their company systems anticipating technologies that would not materialize for years. I then put my plan in a drawer. Every couple of years I took my plan out and revised it based on changes in technology and my maturing ideas. For example, I was responsible for order entry and physical distribution among other applications. In the mid-1970s I converted many of the copies of invoices, shipping documents, and sales reports to microfiche. This meant that salesmen would now have to carry around a microfiche reader-printer, a cumbersome piece of hardware, which required also paper and printer ink.

But I could send documents and reports to the field within a few days instead of a couple of weeks, saving time, postage, and storage. More important, my concept would pave the way for the application I was really interested in, namely, a total customer data base which would include correspondence, salesmen's comments and other uncomputerizable (at the time word processing was unavailable) documentation, etc. The computers the salesmen would eventually carry around would replace the microfiche reader-printers and provide instantaneous access to all customer information.

Later, in the 1980s, when I worked for Peat, Marwick, Mitchell & Co., I became more interested in the computer industry as a whole. I began to realize that consulting would best be accomplished by groups of specialists rather than generalists assembled for that one project. It was then that I began to see the industry as it would be in the future with IBM being only one of the players and not the largest. Combining these into an insight led me to the point which I discuss at length in the book.

Trying to sell what many considered bad news eventually led to the end of my career in computing, however. First, I tried to sell it to Digital Equipment Corporation who wanted to pass IBM as the world's largest computer company, through selling "systems integration" projects. But they wanted to manage projects with the same people they had sold as individual contributors, a very different skill. Instead of putting men in charge of the business in the Atlanta area where I was then ensconced, the local office hired a man who had no experience beyond being an internal project manager in a large company. That was like hiring a cook to command an infantry battalion.

Digital totally mishandled both me and my ideas. I grew so frustrated at seeing my ideas misinterpreted that I started looking for an alternative elsewhere. Out of desperation, I joined a parallel computing entrepreneurial venture, realizing that the secret to success in the consulting business lay in taking on a complex project requiring many different skills. That company, Paralex by name, at first succeeded but owing to the megalomania of the principal, the venture suddenly collapsed after a year. That experience taught me the dynamics of the scientific end of computer industry, most of which holds true today and much of which is little understood. I tried to sell my ideas for a single application business for a few more years with little success. I was able to try my ideas again with a company whose sales manager was very interested in my program, but whose CEO was very unsupportive and scuttled the whole effort.

I suppose all these successes and disasters were helped along by my degree in English and my many years of reading important literature and a wide variety of non-fiction on many, sometimes abstruse subjects. This led me to acquire a high degree of critical reasoning—and beyond that to a unique sort of imagination that worked. Critical reasoning is worthless without experience and an intuition allayed by skepticism.

Research is not enough. Ideology is baseless. My elaborate form of reasoning I like to call prophetic, because with it you can sometimes figure out what people will do in the future based on the dynamics of their personalities while working with others. The interrelationship of personalities impinges upon the present and most probable future and the situation you and they find yourselves today and for the foreseeable future. It's very like writing a novel over which the author has no control (The greatest writers do not work from a plan but allow the story to form organically out of the logic of the characters and situations. I have written many stories).

Being a visionary was not always an advantage, however, because business managers usually prefer someone who is more ordinary, superior in degree and not in kind. And as my track record of holding a job became worse and worse, the suspicion grew that I was some kind of loose cannon, especially as I told a story that meant such a radical change in the common perception.

Even my ability to communicate with senior corporate management and my $300 suits became a disadvantage. When the engineers took over, they saw me as not technical enough, an "empty suit". They didn't like the fact that I could explain things without jargon. Or that I wasn't the least bit interested in the latest and greatest whizbang of a theory for project management or technical development. Most often I discovered that the glossy new idea was like putting old wine in new bottles; something I'd already figured out and was using. But the average technician loved "new" ideas; that way they didn't have to think about how to do things. Some guru had already done it for them.

Which brings me to this book. You might expect a straightforward linear narrative, beginning at the beginning and ending at the end. That is not my intent. I will start at the time I realized I had failed, then discuss the core of my ideas, and why they failed to gain traction, concluding with the beginning of IBM's decline, why it occurred and what that had to do with my own failure.

The period of IBM's decline was probably the most momentous period in the history of computing, even more than the re-invention of the Personal Computer as a piece of consumer electronics. It meant a radical change in the entire computer industry, a change whose influence is still being felt. For one thing it opened the door to technologies and business entities not controlled by Big Blue. This in turn led to the infinite variety of computer businesses we know of today, many of which cropped up overnight. Even though IBM tried to control the PC business, it failed to do so. And this is part of the story, too.

Then I recount the After in which my prophecies came true and my numerous misapprehensions also appeared. This is the time when Personal Computers became a piece of consumer electronics with a power far exceeding that of the previous generation of mainframes. It was the era of the Internet boom and bust. This in turn led to the chaotic state of the current industry where applications and "platforms" beat general purpose computing every time. And where software is so much the king of the hill that an entrepreneur such as Gates or Zuckerberg can make a mint without sacrificing too much of a company to venture capitalists and IPOS (unlike the hardware vendors). The Internet has become the dominant computer-based technology (although a mixed blessing at best), where mainframes have given way to server systems, where Personal Computers have replaced engineering workstations, and where tablets threaten to obliterate Personal Computers. Where a relative newcomer such as Samsung can undersell Apple in the latter's own marketplace. Where platforms such as the Ipad that integrate software and hardware into a specialized bundle is the future of technology.

Because computer applications tend to spring from the minds of very young people, some in their teens, the innovative new companies are dominated by people in their twenties and thirties. Almost all these companies are run by engineers and programmers, very different from the time when salesmen and MBAs ruled the roost. The computer pioneers of the 1980s and early 1990s are, for the most part, still with us. Some, like Bill Gates, are middle-aged. Others, like Zuckerberg, are a whole generation younger. From the very stable industry of the first thirty years of its existence, the mid-to-late eighties sea change has migrated to an era where nothing is certain – and every company, including Microsoft, Apple, Oracle,

Intel can become obsolescent in a flash. Thus, I will tell this story right up to the time of the beginning of the social network and how this relates to my observations way back in the 1980s.

Another reason I chose this particular era is because this is in the end a very personal book – and what can be more personally consequential than the collapse of a career. It is a time when I began to think deeply about a variety of subjects, some much wider than technology. Push it deep enough and the Why? becomes a very big question, one that has implications far beyond one's self.

And because the era was also the beginning of a time of profound social change, the book is about the social, political, and psychological factors that were both the cause and the effect of IBM's decline and the collapse of my career. For the world looked very different in the early 1980s then it does today. The sixties did not fail, it only morphed. For most of us, the 1980s looked more like the 1940s then they do the 2010s.

I will also briefly provide a history of the time before the Great Watershed. This will cover a lot of ground comparatively quickly. The purpose here is to contrast the origin of the industry with its current state. Here, I plan to begin with my introduction to the computer industry in 1965. Still very early but not the absolute beginning. Not that I will ignore entirely the early days of the industry and the emergence of IBM as the single absolute power.

I will proceed through my years as an internal data processor with attention to the gradually changing structure and dynamics of the industry and how that affected the way computer people did things – and my frustration at not being allowed to make the organizational changes necessary to accommodate the much larger and more complex systems of the future. I will briefly cover my years as a Big Eight (then) accounting firm management consultant, a very different career path than my time as an internal data processing manager. And my first attempt to sell my ideas at Digital Equipment Corporation. I will conclude with a brief synopsis of the computer industry since the time of my decline in the industry and the personal factors that made it impossible for me to succeed.

CHAPTER ONE

MY BUSINESS CAREER WANES

I feel a special urgency in writing this book, an urgency that comes from sensing something about my past that also reveals something poorly understood about the history of the computer industry. Something that explains the course of my life, but that has implications for you and anybody else affected by the computer industry. That is, everybody except maybe for those neo-Luddites such as I have become, who'd just as soon most computer technology would go away.

For the last twenty years I have tried to drag a tiny bit of wisdom out of my subconscious (if you believe a subconscious is possible), order it, and write it all down, applying all the concentration I could muster. I often lost myself for days at a time. The result – thousands of pages of unpublishable text.

I have often thought I should give it up. Perhaps the things I have to say aren't all that important. Or if they are, someone else, someone smarter and more talented, will have made the same discoveries I have made and written them down clearer and better than I can.

And I could have been mistaken. What I thought was illumination may have only been swamp gas. I could have wasted the last productive years of my life on a will-o-the wisp.

Nah. Nobody thinks like I do.

The computer industry isn't known for its articulate souls and philosophical thinkers. And I've got that in spades. I love to wrestle with ideas and the implications of those ideas. The reason my ideas have been unpublishable is I haven't figured out exactly how to express my them. Until now.

Besides, writing is inherently a lonely business, a lot like programming. Except that it's social. Every writer hopes and expects to win an audience. Programmers really only care about their own end product.

Besides, it's natural to get the heebie-jeebies when you experience a lot of rejection. I've got a large file folder full of those kinds of letters. But I've got to believe if anybody can express my ideas, I can.

In spite of all the failure and self-doubt; in spite of the elusiveness and impermanence of truth itself, I am convinced that there is something fundamental that I have been allowed to glimpse, something that can be given extension and weight, something that matters. And there is progress, my work today is more coherent than that of yesterday, and more complex. The words flow faster now. There are fewer rocky places, fewer shoals.

And miracle of miracles, I have recently published a book on *politics,* of all things, to almost universal acclaim… so far. If I can do *that,* surely I can write about something I know a lot about.

But there is so little time. I am 76 now and by the time this is finished I'll be 77. Will I ever see this book published? Will there be an audience if I do?

oOo

I suppose to it's natural for me to think back to the day nearly twenty-five years ago when I embarked on this unlikely Odyssey. What was I thinking back then? How, when I have never particularly admired intellectuals and their airy reasoning, did I develop this burning need to express myself this way? Why did I throw myself so enthusiastically into this angst-ridden marginal activity that can hardly be labeled a career?

Part of the reason should be obvious to people in the literary business. If you want to be a writer you invariably long to write the Great American Novel or some approximation thereof. Unless you're a genre writer, e.g. thrillers, romance novels, sci fi, you have to be really, really good to get anywhere, especially if you are on the far edges of literary fiction. Why do you think there are so many competent novelists on the faculty of small colleges in Nowheresville, USA? Because the pyramid of literature is very steep, very slippery, and very narrow at the top.

I discovered early on that my goal of being a great fiction writer had a couple of major obstacles. One, I had little interest in the vagaries of my characters. What I liked was ideas. And forcing my ideas into stories was next to impossible. And second, I had a tin ear for dialogue. Not that any of it was awful, mind you. But I thought you had to make it sound like real people talking. Which flat doesn't work. Dialogue, just like everything else in a story has to move the narrative along.

Now, you might have guessed there is a story worth telling about my fiction-writing career, but that's for another time.

The proximate cause of this quasi-memoir is easy to identify. One day as I was idling away at a job that I detested, a terrifying anxiety came over me. Instead of converting a body shop consulting outfit into a projects business, I had been relegated to selling individual techies out of an office overlooking Colony Square in Atlanta, Georgia. To me this was a boring and unrewarding job and if you think of a job that way there's no way you're going to be anything but mediocre at it.

But the feeling I had that afternoon was more intense than that. It began with a sense that I was suddenly coming down with an illness. I shivered as from a chill, became faint and a little nauseous. I perspired profusely. But the more intense my feelings became, the more I realized that this was no disease.

Now, I have often been subject to night terrors. I am by nature a rabbit who masquerades as a lion. And two A.M. is the hour when all the suppressed anxiety boils up from my subconscious. When Napoleon wrote about two o'clock in the morning courage this is what he was fighting against. So this feeling was not unfamiliar to me. But this time I was awake and the feeling of terror was many times as intense as I had ever felt.

I became convinced that if I looked up from the stack of papers cluttering my desk, I would see a hooded figure pointing a spindly finger at me and about to speak. You have failed, the figure would tell me, and not just in the immediate sense, but in the ultimate Calvinist one. This is it, you have misused your talents, there are no more chances.

I don't know if you've ever had a feeling like this, but it is a little like death. Even the most committed atheist doesn't want to think that her life is entirely devoid of meeting. And that's what I was admitting.

Now I'm far too much of a rationalist to have ever experienced anything like a mystical revelation and this sense of a metaphysical presence only added to my sense of foreboding. Was I losing my grip? The tension was unbearable. I had to do something. I forced myself to look up. And, of course nothing was there.

The terror immediately dissipated. It was as though I had been granted a reprieve. I took a deep breath, gathered myself and tried to get back to work.

And, truth be known, my feeling of depression was a red herring. I am given to melancholy, but I am nothing if not persistent. There were other jobs and other careers ahead of me and my best work has only now begun. Nobody's done for unless they want to be.

Nevertheless, on that day a nagging anxiety remained, a mosquito bite of dissatisfaction, which itched and festered into an unbearable aggravation. Soon I found myself unable to concentrate even to the trifling degree required by my job. I had been working all day on a proposal for an air crew scheduling system for Delta Air Lines, the kind of system I'd done a dozen times before.

I told you mundane computer work was boring.

I began to think about what had just happened. I dropped my pencil on the pad of lined paper that lay across my desk.

I had screwed up my career, that much was undeniable. But how could I possibly think myself a failure in any ultimate sense? I was still in my forties and a middle manager at that. Isn't it true that there had been times, and recently too, that I had been recognized for exceptional performance? I'll admit that this job isn't working out the way I hoped, but I am in no danger of losing it.

And even if I should decide that this work isn't for me, even should I decide to leave consulting altogether, would that be the end of things? I have other experience. There has to be a career out there to which I am better suited; another company where I would feel more at home. I only have to find it. Why by any normal yardstick, I'm just doing fine.

Or so I rationalized. But in all this positive thinking I could not deny a simple and devastating truth: at the age of forty-six, I was whatever I was going to be. Promise, the one element that had always been my trademark was forever gone. And without promise, I would be limited by my qualifications, by my education and experience to a *job*, that is, to somebody else's perception of what I ought to be. Henceforth, I would most likely be squeezed, I shuddered at the thought, into a routine and bureaucratic *position* where some time-server would try to manage me into submission.

A fate worse than death? Hardly. Most people have jobs that are routine and unchallenging. Lives of quiet desperation. Was I better than them? Sure seems like I thought so. Wasn't that a little arrogant?

So while pushing myself away from my desk, I told myself that this is a complicated world where success is never predictable. How could I have been expected to know how it all would turn out? How much am I responsible for what has happened to me? And if I am not responsible for my fate, when it is not I who failed but circumstances.

This wasn't a good answer, either. And I knew it as soon as I thought it. And so I turned my swivel chair around, stood up and looked out the window toward the Lenox Square shopping center, my eyes losing focus as I sank into a dreamlike state that comes to me when I am in a state of absolute concentration. And as often happens when something I poorly understand tugs away at my conscience, my mind began to churn reflexively. I knew that I was in for a long afternoon.

What I didn't realize then was that afternoon would only be the beginning, that the entire remainder of my life would turn on that brief moment of anxiety.

I shook my head to disperse my reverie. Focus, I told myself, focus. And my churning consciousness began to come around to concepts. Not very poetic, I'll admit, but who wants to stop at poetry when the world is so filled with tangles to be unwoven.

Sure, my reasoning continued, I have made some mistakes out of pure, hardheaded cussedness. I have been all too willing to succumb to thought when action was required. I was aggressive when I should have been passive, and reluctant when I should have pushed ahead. And other lapses of character. But didn't everyone have similar flaws? Then why did I feel so disconsolate at what had happened to me?

Because I couldn't shake the conviction that the responsibility for my life was mine and mine alone. If there were problems in my career, it was because I had failed to avoid them.

I'm not so naïve as to believe that a person is entirely in control of his own fate; life is too complex a proposition to be certain of what the future will bring, no matter how well you plan it. But you can, I am convinced, anticipate and influence events to some degree and the result of that influence goes somewhere and has meaning. Any other way of thinking and I would be nothing more than a cork bobbing on an endless sea.

Helpless determinism has always been intolerable to me – and is no less so now. And if I can't accept the mechanical explanation this implies now when I have become almost all thought and don't actually do anything, there was no way that, in my mid-forties back then and in the midst of an aggressively pursued career, I was going to let myself succumb to that kind of passivity. Succeed or fail, I had taken action. I was responsible for it all.

Then how, I wondered how had it come to this pass? I'm an intelligent fellow, look good in a business suit, inspire confidence.

No obvious answer came to mind. No matter how much I thought about it from a purely historical examination, no satisfactory answer was ever going to come.

I suppose I could have told myself that this was just one of those complicated riddles that made life a mystery and gotten back to work. But I have always been given to self-examination and believed back then that there was no problem without a solution.

I began to look beyond events for reasons for my difficulties, Something that couldn't be seen through an examination of personality or events. Something both inside and outside me. And here's what came to me:

For quite some time and through several jobs, even those where I achieved a modicum of success, I sensed that there was a disconnection between the job I was hired to do and the job I felt I should be doing. It was a feeling that was more than the feeling of inadequacy that haunts most people from time to time. I knew the kind of job I should be doing and yet I could never seem to find anyone to hire me to do it.

At the very end of this book I will discuss a couple of opportunities I had in real businesses where I was very successful on the surface but that ended badly for me nevertheless.

But what did that mean in the context of my life? Had it been a mistake for me to take the jobs I *could* get and try to make the best of them? Or was my discontent the mistake? Wouldn't I have been better off accepting the world's assessment of my abilities and letting it go at that? Or should I have continued battling along this seemingly impossible front until I at last broke through?

CHAPTER TWO

THE PECULIAR WAY I RELATE TO THE WORLD

What are my abilities I asked myself, adding, and what do they mean in both the context of myself and the world at large?

Under the best of circumstances, those were no simple questions. What's more, I had never confronted any of them before. And so my convoluted mental processes began cranking away in a new and still more tedious direction.

Because my mind is cluttered with an accumulation of almost every fact or idea of consequence I have encountered during my entire life, I tend to go through a stripping process until I come to a single point of focus. Sometimes this single focus is the conclusion I seek and sometimes only a step along the way to the conclusion. Until I have tested my hypothesis, I can never know which. If I decide (usually after a painfully soul-searching analysis) that I have not found the answer yet, I return to the stripping process now taking into account the fallacies and any new implications I have discovered the first time. And I repeat the process again and again until I am completely satisfied that I'm close to understanding.

I might add here that no answer is absolutely final. We must repeatedly challenge our most cherished beliefs. We must seek out new opinions, ideas, and facts, even those that are disagreeable to our way of thinking. This is the reason I despise ideologies and distrust thinkers that accept pat answers and nurture them as they would a much-awaited newborn, never examining contrary opinions. Or, worse, avoiding exposing themselves to unfamiliar ideas altogether.

It should not be surprising that my rumination ran deep into the evening. I suppose my coworkers who slipped out the door one after the other mistakenly believed I was working myself to death.

I stayed there into the early morning boiling my thoughts down to a conclusion as to the one characteristic that more than any other defines my way of reasoning, but which until that moment I had never given a name.

For want of a better word, I decided to call it prophecy. Though not in the sense of foretelling the future, but in the Biblical sense of understanding the nature of things, not just how they appear but what in essence they are. In the Bible, of course the prophets are only channels and the source of this insight is Yahweh.

Prophecy is a characteristic I have to some degree possessed since I was a small child, but has been transformed by my social insecurities into my own peculiar way of dealing with the world.

I have not always dealt with the world the way I do today. During my childhood I would become so frustrated when my team lost that I would throw things at the wall or yell and scream. My mother would tell her friends, "Michael is *so* dramatic." Unfortunately, her friends were the parents of my friends, and I became the butt of "so dramatic" jokes well into my teenage years. That taught me a lesson I have never forgotten. You'd better be careful when you reveal characteristics that may be received negatively.

Yet this psychic branding poured into other things that made me a bit of an outcast. From my earliest days I was afraid of many things. Thunder, barking dogs, heights, even exotic plants. Although I conquered all these fears by my teenage years, my skittishness still marked me out as different from other boys. Further, I was not very athletic. Not terrible, mind you, but bad enough so that I was usually chosen near the end. Athletes were and are at the top of the social heap in and out of school, and, unfortunately, I was constantly cast into situations where athleticism was the be-all and end-all. I went to a camp every summer for five years where the owner was a college baseball coach. The "well-rounded boy" was admired; the Rhodes scholar type was especially admired. I became the designated scorekeeper.

My Dad, who admired athletes, was a locally-ranked tennis player as a boy. He, an award-winning salesman himself, once told me I should never be a salesman because I couldn't work up the courage to apply for a summer job in an engineering firm. Their newspaper advertisement said they wanted an engineering major and I was not that. I was convinced I would wind up making a fool of myself but my Dad was convinced I could sell myself if I wanted to.

In high school from which I graduated in record time, my one activity outside of study was the "eraser committee."

And then I went to the Virginia Military Institute. In some ways, VMI was a horrible experience. I only lasted two years and I was near the bottom of the pecking order the whole time.

But I will be eternally grateful to the school for teaching me how to keep my head down and merge with the crowd by suppressing my more objectionable characteristics. I joined a fraternity when I transferred to the University of Virginia and had many friends there.

The cost of my acquired adaptability was that I had to be very careful about what I said or did. In unfamiliar situations I was always guarded. My fraternity high-jinks were always half-hearted. But nobody noticed. To those few I became really close to, however, they remarked on a certain stiffness.

Social awkwardness is a common trait, especially among the kind of men who are more comfortable with the predictability of machines than the infinite variety of human nature. But I have grown competent in social situations and my insecurity does not occur out of an excess of logic. Mine arises out of oversensitivity toward the inner feelings of others –their self-absorption as well as their generosity – an empathy so intense that is sometimes physically painful to me. The sense of pure, unthought-out emotion is excruciating, while the baser drives – anger, cruelty, lust – are terrifying. And emotional spontaneity, alarming.

The only way I have found to cope with my hypersensitivity is to convert my emotional reaction into an understanding that I can then verbalize. Then I can relate it to the matter at hand. If I sense there is too much at stake emotionally, I will make some temporizing remark so that I can have more time to think about the situation, sometimes agonizing over it for days at a time.

By this means I can appear to be reasonable while seething inside. Although I may be painfully in tune with the emotional being of others, I can appear cold and unfeeling.

There is a downside to my analytical sensitivity, I am often accused of being difficult to read. And since people don't trust others they can't immediately size up, I have made few long-term friends. For it is through emotional feedback that we reach a character judgment and it is through character judgment that we are able to conclude if another person is someone we wish to grow close to.

I can't say I'm happy about the common assessment of me, but I'm not about to change my style. I would far rather be misunderstood than express a spontaneous emotion I will later regret. I think I'm fairer in my judgments of my associates than if I expressed my immediate reaction to what they said or did. And fairer still to the new people I encounter, because by this method I avoid the stereotyping which forms most first impressions and which is too often our ultimate judgment as well.

What my method did not allow me to do was to penetrate beneath the surface of human motivations to the existential causes of it all. This I would only discover after I took up writing.

oOo

This is not an uncomplicated way of thinking. The longer I know a person, the more tangled are the threads of my understanding about him and the longer it takes to weave a new intuition among those I already possessed. And so I spend much of my life deep in thought and am often by myself even when I am not alone.

How little of my life has been spent living in the conventional sense! How infrequently have I allowed immediate reality to penetrate into my inner world!

If not deep in thought, I am likely to be found buried in a book. As an adult I have read five thousand or more of them. History, social criticism, the natural and social sciences, a little philosophy. And, oh, yes, fiction of a certain quality. Everything for self-improvement and always in the quest of meaning.

But why, when an understanding of life means to have experienced it, do I reflexively turn to books?

Because the world in books is orderly and predictable and abstracted into truths – at least that's what the author hopes to accomplish. In the psychology, sociology, criticism and theorizing of non-fiction lie the reasons why people are the way they are, ready-made and without the need to reason them through. And in fiction lies a representation of the mind and soul of the author that can be related to the minds and souls of people you know. Or your own. You can never know the inner being of another as well as you can that of a master story-teller. That is, if you pay close attention.

oOo

This then is how I deal with a single human being I might encounter:

All the disparate impressions of her congeal and form over minutes, hours, days. And then somewhere in my mind it all comes together, the symptoms of character as expressed in her reactions, her general demeanor becoming an understanding. Is she timid, arrogant, sweet-natured, hostile? All this allows me to form an idea as to who she might be. This I will combine with previous impressions of other people and the observations about similar persons I find in books. Then and only then do I feel comfortable with reacting to the person or situation.

And, yes, I'll admit it. I can be unspontaneous. Although not as often as you might imagine. For this same method of reason can allow me to prepare for situations which have not yet occurred. Once I get to know a person, I can often predict how she will react to something I might do or say and then prepare a plan as to how to deal with that reaction. Being aware of the likely course of events in advance of their occurrence, I can structure my personality to take advantage of it (or minimize the damage).

This careful, self-protective way of dealing with the world is not as uncommon as you might think. It is often found in literary figures. Proust is an extreme example of such an analytical sensitive. But it is highly unusual in the sometimes brutal arena of human affairs. And as to business…well, I realize now that it took almost unbelievable drive (or perverted insecurity) for me to accomplish anything there.

oOo

Once committed to a business career, however, I discovered that there were uses that could be made of my odd way of dealing with my fellow man. Since organizations are human creations and obey the same psychological laws as those that apply to individuals, it was possible for me to discern the inner psychology of a business in the same way I could understand that of a person I might know. In this way, I could see patterns in the ebb and flow of human activity in the large where others only saw chaos, and predictability.

And since the inner logic of larger groups of people is even more abstracted than that of individual people and more transparent, they are also more predictable. Thus, I could foresee business and social trends long before they manifested themselves in reality.

Here again my readings, most particularly in history, combined with my life's experience, allowed me to reach conclusions as to what was about to happen and why.

History has been particularly helpful to me because the events of history, endlessly repeated and yet with development and change, can allow me to understand what is different this time. Also, the process of writing history with its focus on cause and effect served as a means to test my predictions logically.

This made me something of a prophet in the other sense of being able to foretell the future. But too often I was a prophet without honor, especially early in my career, and most especially those thirteen years when I was a Systems Analyst and later a Data Processing Manager at A.H. Robins, a fortune 600 pharmaceutical company in Richmond, VA. To most of my peers and superiors, on the whole an unimaginative lot, I was an odd duck whose observations were often at odds with their own preconceptions. It didn't help that the events I foresaw always – or most always –happened as I thought they would and had the consequences I expected them to. No one likes a Cassandra even when her predictions are true and might have avoided disaster (*especially* if they could have avoided disaster). Besides, what twenty to thirty-year- old could possibly possess such wisdom as I claimed to have. I came to be regarded as arrogant, negative, and pessimistic. Even when my logic agreed with theirs.

It soon became clear that my capabilities were useful only so long as I used them indirectly. I would have to manipulate people and events instead of revealing what I understood. At A.H.Robins personality was always more prized than ability. The back-slapping country club type, members of the softball and basketball teams, were most rewarded. And intellectuals (which meant anyone who had any kind of inner life) were regarded as fuzzy-thinking and impractical, a view which I, being young and insecure, came to accept. After all, to paraphrase E. Clairborne Robins, Senior, anybody can do any job, so why not promote your friends.

I kept my talents a secret, while producing many tangible accomplishments in an attempt to prove that I was a practical fellow after all. And I hoped, vainly as it would turn out, that by building a wall of accomplishments I would never be fired.

Eventually, though, the strain of suppressing the truth of my inner self proved too much to manage and in the early eighties the inevitable crisis occurred. I was put against the wall by a project manager who knew nothing about managing projects and a back-stabbing peer who had spread lies about me for years. I was forced to leave A.H.Robins shortly after my thirty-ninth birthday.

oOo

After a brief period of semi-employment as a contract consultant for a small, local startup, I took a job as a senior consultant with

Peat Marwick Mitchell & Co., one of the then Big Eight public accounting firms.

My four-and-a-half years at Peat Marwick were a wholly different experience from that at A.H.Robins. While most of my consulting projects involved rigorous and often tedious analyses according to a predefined plan of work, there was still some play for the imagination. Intellect of any sort was prized. I worked the college and university circuit and sprinkling my presentations with quotations from literature and history had a big impact. Far from being discouraged, insight was one of the ways to get ahead. The most successful consultants seemed to be the ones who had the ability to take some original concept and package it into a service.

And I thought to myself: It's actually possible to make a living off of understanding things! I could do that. I looked around for a patch of still water on which to cast my net. I soon began to find things I could do to improve my value as a consultant, simple things for the most part, small improvements to existing processes.

This was the way that ninety percent of my peers built their own practices. Which only made sense, since the world is improved by small modifications to existing systems not radical change.

But the partner I worked for kept a tight rein on my efforts. It's true he was much better than I was as a bush-beating salesman. But he could at least have given my ideas the time of day.

And besides the little improvements seemed so mundane somehow and I was boundlessly ambitious. Soon my insights took on a grandiose and universal quality. And as my concepts became larger and more abstract, they also became more complicated.

The story of my life.

CHAPTER THREE

THE INSIGHT OF A LIFETIME

There was an idea that took hold of my mind, fascinated me, and yet seemed simple enough to form the raw material for the rest of my career. An idea so powerful that I had spent the five years previous to my epiphany trying to make capital out of it.

That idea went something like this: In the mid to late 1980s the computer industry was in the midst of a sea change and the old rules were about to be shattered and in some cases reversed.

The dominant force in the industry, the International Business Machines Company (IBM), was beginning to flounder. Its strategies were in direct conflict with emerging market realities. For example, the core of IBM's technology, its mainframe business, was threatened with obsolescence. And IBM was not the market leader in a number of fast-growing industry segments – personal computing, networking, and distributed processing among others. Corporate managements were demanding much more complex and sophisticated system features, many requiring capabilities IBM did not then support.

Internal computer departments were, therefore, having to struggle with a radical new technical reality without the traditional crutch provided by IBM's marketing and technical support. Many of them had no inkling of where to start. Inevitably, I believed, most would look for help from those computer industry firms that seemed to have a logical answer; those that had lived off of IBM's way of doing computing, but recognized the need for change. Which meant,

I was convinced, that those firms were going to have to provide more than just hardware *or* software *or* the systems development services that they had heretofore offered, but all three at once. They were going to have to provide total "solutions."

And I knew how this could be done.

Now, foreseeing a trend is one thing, making something out of it quite another. Fortunately for me, I had learned a few management skills along the way. How to write a proposal or a business plan, for example. These, along with my wide exposure to many areas of the industry, allowed me to both form the concepts I was selling, and apply some structure to them as well. I had also acquired the promotional skills to market ideas from my brief stint as an entrepreneur.

Here's how I came to believe as I did:

During my years as a management consultant, I had observed a large number of internal computer departments, every one of which was wrestling with the increasing sophistication of the technology with which they worked, and in particular with the process required to implement a new version of the bet-your-business applications, such as manufacturing or wholesale distribution.

Building a completely new system that had all the features of the old plus the new features required to run a modern business was no trivial problem: a major implementation project in a medium-sized company might occupy several years of full-time effort on the part of a number of people with several different skills and an investment that might run into the millions of dollars.

Deciphering all the old features was one major problem since no two programmers attacked a problem the same way and legacy systems ten, fifteen, or more years old were usually filled with poorly documented and confusing, "spaghetti" code, making deciphering it still more impossible. As a consequence, nobody knew exactly how the old system worked…or could find out.

But the hardest part of replacement systems was incorporating the new breed of strategic capabilities. No longer was the goal merely automating the back-office functions of the business, but increasingly at improving the competitive position of the enterprise as a whole. The new breed of systems was much more comprehensive in business function and much more technically complex as well. Thus, they were far more difficult to implement. But because of their strategic importance, the pressure to install the new way in a year or two was immense.

Internal computer staffs were of little assistance in this process. Few of their people had ever been through a major implementation project. And those that had, grizzled veterans of the fifties and sixties, had experience that in no way qualified them to work on the new order of things. Back then, the implementation process had been quite crude; a few programmers could muddle their way through to a system which was expected to last two or three years at the most. And wound up being patched together for ten or fifteen.

Furthermore, they were written and modified for just the new features by people who often didn't write the original programs. This was tedious work in which minor changes might require months of testing and retesting and further modification. There was little or no documentation concerning the original design or about any of the modifications made all those years and those programmers and analysts with memories long enough to recall a piece of the application invariably knew it in a technical way that had little to do with real user needs. In the end, no one knew exactly how the applications worked or why.

Nor did the internal staffs have the necessary knowledge of the software products around which the new systems were to be based. Furthermore, vendor training and support, at best perfunctory, was grossly inadequate. They expected internal staffs to figure out what to do with a few days training centered around huge, cryptic tomes which purported to be training manuals and were so full of detail that it was almost impossible to glean the company's needs from them.

Worse than the inexperience and lack of knowledge of the internal implementation staffs was the almost total absence of project managers to run such an endeavor. The skills required for project management are very different from those necessary to be a day-to-day manager of an operational computer function – and far, far different from those of most user department supervisors.

Nor was project management a skill that was easy to train someone to possess, since a competent project manager should have not only a knowledge of the software she is about to use and prior experience in the implementation of that software, but certain rarely found personal characteristics as well. These included extraordinary attention to detail, mental toughness to live under pressure for long periods of time and the sensitivity to recognize when the project is off track. Most of all, the leadership to motivate a team with a wide variety of skills and personalities.

The sort of visionary person, who does the planning to implement system capabilities is very different from the straw boss who actually runs the project. The technicians who do the programming, software installation, and equipment selection and installation – required several different types of knowledge and experience. These would have very different personalities and skills from the conceptualizers and managers. Then there are the user team members who must live with the end products but who often know just enough about the technical aspects to be dangerous. If internal computer departments had been struggling to maintain the traditional applications, they were overwhelmed by the idea of the new kind. And this without the kind of support they had traditionally expected from IBM.

These realities presented a huge business opportunity for an integrated "solutions" company.

Imagine, if you will, a company that specializes in the implementation of one particular application, say, wholesale distribution. Such a company could hire specialists who know the capabilities of the most up-to-date software, and others who are expert in the machinery and business organization required to install that application. It could manage these employees through project methodologies tailor-made for that type of business problem. And it could use its staff's experience in many other similar implementations to improve the efficiency and predictability of the process. In ten or twenty years the employees of such a company would have completed dozens of implementations, not just one.

A company organized this way could implement a business system better, faster, and maybe cheaper than any internal computer department. In an era when computer regimes were being replaced every few years, often owing to some calamitous project failure, a solutions business could almost guarantee success.

oOo

But this was not the way the computer industry was organized. Structured into pockets of expertise and product, often wrestling with the conflict between generalists and specialists, the industry was at best offering fragmented "point" solutions.

Not that there was no one attempting to address the customer's total problem. The large national consulting organizations, such as Arthur Andersen (now named Accenture), had been offering themselves as "systems integrators" since the early days of the industry. But they were trying to do this with the same old methodologies that they had invented to address individual applications, a very different dynamic than that was then emerging. For while information systems now required very technical *specialists*, the large consulting organizations favored *generalists* with soft, management-oriented skills. Andersen, for example, regarded the entire field of systems development as its bailiwick: its Method/One implementation technique was generalized for all types of applications and was primarily procedural. They were famous for staffing their projects with what was known in the industry as the "Kiddie Corps". These were recent MBAs, who had no knowledge of the technical aspect of computing or even the applications to which they were assigned. I was a consultant for what was then known as Peat Marwick Mitchell & Co. Although I had many years of designing, installing, and enhancing one of the most sophisticated integrated wholesale distribution systems in the industry, I wound up working the Higher Education circuit, because my original manager specialized in that arena. Sort of reminds you of the draftee who graduated from college as an Electrical Engineer being assigned as a company clerk.

While there were pockets of both technical and management focus within these giant national firms, these arose out of a Darwinian process where you fit in where the management needed you to be. If you could adapt, you could be successful. The "up or out" method of winnowing out misfits meant that those who made the partnership were mainly good salesmen. The really good imaginative or technical consultants were usually not good salesmen and eventually had to seek greener pastures. Those few technicians that could sell well enough to make the partnership found that they were spending most of their time cosseting clients while their skills eroded.

These firms were also very expensive to hire with average billing rates in the mid-1980s of $100 per hour or more. Some consulting firms offered software products to support the new type of systems. Those few that did only addressed certain niches. Peat Marwick had a bunch of code that supported State Government accounting, for example, but it had to be extensively modified for each state. After all, the main reason for large national consulting firms was the profitable sale of consulting services.

And these firms stayed as far away from equipment as they could, usually depending on IBM for that expertise. Andersen's Method/One was designed around IBM technology for this reason. As we shall see, IBM-based projects were especially difficult to manage.

Too many consultant-led projects had, as a consequence, failed, usually after huge sums of money had been spent and reams of worthless paper produced. And those that *did* manage to be implemented, did so only after many target dates had passed and with huge cost overruns.

oOo

I do not wish to understate the difficulty of converting a consulting business to the provision of total solutions rather than merely development projects. To acquire the infrastructure to market and execute projects require a very sophisticated organization, unlike that of any of the firms I targeted for my ideas. Solutions projects were very complex and notoriously risky to undertake. Few small businesses (and most of the IBM-related software firms were quite small) would be willing to bet-the-business on a pig in the poke I proposed unless the business case were overwhelming.

I knew, however, that an integrated solutions approach was not only possible, it was the best way to run any software and/or services firm. The case was so strong I was certain I could persuade the executives of such businesses of that fact.

The key to the whole problem and the core of my argument against the status quo was Project Management. Competent project managers are even more essential when you are attempting to run the project as a consultant rather than as an employee. This is because there is less flexibility in budget and time projections. If you fix bid a project, you'd better get it right the first time.

Project managers, however, are a rare breed, more born than trained. Success is based on control of the project process from the very beginning of the sale to the final sign-off, meaning he or she must understand all phases of the project and be able to communicate that to technicians and corporate managers alike. I have seen perhaps six competent project managers in my career, and dozens of bad ones.

Fortunately for my proposal, project managers are easier to find and retain in a consulting business than in an internal department, because the pay and status are much higher in the former.

Since they will be the face of the project to the client, project managers cannot also be project salesmen, whose responsibility should end with the close of the deal. Luckily, most salesmen welcome the presence of a project manager on the sales team. If the project manager is socially and technically competent, he will be adept at gaining the confidence of his prospective clients and can largely sell themselves. Further, unlike most salesmen he actually likes the administrative details required to produce a proposal, a process that is also a project with procedures and deliverables.

Project managers specializing in a single application can minimize project costs by calling for the technical and business specialists and resources required only as they are needed.

(What, you might ask, of all the technical specialists I mentioned earlier? As hard as some of them are to find, wouldn't you need to hire them in anticipation of the project? Not necessarily. An established computer services firm usually has enough skilled specialists on hand to man a project or two, especially if they are used as advisors and planners only. Or you can begin by subcontracting this kind of work. Most of the day-to-day work can be performed by generalist programmers and systems analysts drawn from the existing consulting company.)

Thus, a company could enter a solutions business by hiring only a couple of project managers – and me – up front, knowing that in six months or so, the only one not generating revenue would be me. The project managers will be billable once the project is begun and sometimes earlier, because it is possible to also bill for project planning. The total upfront investment for this business initiation phase, counting travel expense ought to be a few hundred thousand dollars, a trivial sum by today's standards.

oOo

But that doesn't address the formidable organizational structure necessary to get the business rolling. Just determining all the various skills required is a business problem of the first water. Who knows how many specialized skills are needed, where to get them and for how long?

Then there are the various administrative capabilities required to support the sales and servicing of the business. Project teams require a defined methodology using customized project management software. Marketing materials must be developed so that the sales team looks professional. And there are business partnerships you must form with hardware manufacturers, technical software (e.g. the operating system, the database management system) vendors and other service firms that can serve as subcontractors. Not to speak of the sub-project managers.

And how do you go about finding a person to organize such a complex operation?

Well, there was good news and there was better news (for me, anyway). The good news was that I had most of the organizational capabilities required. I had been an internal data processing manager and a manager of consulting projects and I knew both the conceptual and business side of things. And I already had a plan for how to make it work.

The better news was that there were few others who had the imagination to invent such an enterprise. It would be a long time before I encountered any serious competition.

oOo

Then you had to take into account the risk implicit in any complex implementation project. Rule Number One in business is you should never start a business where the billing unit is too large. Large fixed bid projects can mean a billing unit of tens of thousands of man-hours. Underestimate the man-power requirements and you destroy whatever profitability you anticipated. Overestimate the project and some other firm is likely to underbid you.

Every computer industry executive has experienced or at least heard of consulting firms wrecked by quagmire projects ending in huge losses and law suits. Years before, I had an oh, so poignant, experience in such a disaster myself. Between my stints at A. H. Robins and Peat Marwick I worked for a small consulting company which self-destructed by taking on several projects that were too complex for their limited capabilities.

One of our projects was "managed" by a woman who bore the scars of a slashed wrist. A second employee checked into a "behavioral health center" mid-way through the project. A third was ushered out of a bank because he had once served as a "guest of the state." And we only had seven people on staff.

You really have to be careful in hiring folks.

Even if the employees had been able to complete their assignments, the work was so underbid the company would have gone broke in a matter of months.

"Solution" projects would be especially prone to such an outcome since you are making a fixed bid on a product that is only a concept and implemented reality always falls short of the customer's imagination.

Failure is not inevitable, however. The risk of conflict between customer expectations and consulting firm capabilities can be minimized if you follow a couple of simple rules:

First, you must select your initial projects where there are straightforward and well-defined deliverables and where the customer and his staff are, for the most part, receptive to your presence. While such projects will likely be comparatively small, it is more important to make a little profit safely than it is to try to make a killing by taking on some huge, ill- defined endeavor (for some reason "huge", and "ill-defined" are often synonymous).

Second, you must bid these initial projects on an open-ended, hourly fee basis rather than a fixed fee for the whole project. That way, you can repair any problem in perception on the part of the client or your project manager and still make a profit.

Of course, you must make damn sure you know all the people you hire, not just their paper qualifications, but the content of their character. And when you bid the project you must be sure to build a cushion for turnover and incompetence. There's nothing wrong with beginning your business by hiring contractors from reputable firms when you can't hire people you can be sure of.

oOo

That in a nutshell was what I proposed to do.

It's true that none of these ideas were entirely new to me. There were a few companies already attempting to offer comprehensive turnkey systems. But very few of these competed in the IBM-technology market place and those that did tended to be consulting firms that offered a little software or were software firms that might provide a few services. No one seemed to merge the technical and management problems into a narrow band of solutions the way I did.

In pitching solutions to software and equipment vendors, I believed I was offering the perfect way for companies to overcome and maybe even profit from the impending industry crisis. And I knew how to do it! The wealth and power that might come out of this! It made my head swim!

But brainstorms, no matter how well thought out, must be tempered by the market before they can become a reality. There are obstacles to acceptance that can make the sale of the best business plan more difficult than you could imagine. And unfortunately for me there were a whole Himalayas of barriers to my ideas.

To begin with the mid-1980s when I formed my ideas were good years for the firms that leeched off of IBM technology and my seemingly negative prophecies were most often met not with enthusiasm but with dismay and denial.

So what, my audience reasoned, if growth was beginning to slow. You can't expect to have twenty percent growth every year. Why, for those who had been around then, we remember when IBM plateaued in the early fifties, just before they began to build computers.

What if I was right and things get dicey later on? There are a wide variety of strategies that don't involve such radical changes as I proposed. Such as going after new or closely related markets.

But what, I argued, if the closely-related markets didn't exist? Or they were going through the same sort of decline you are? What if the new markets are so radically different from the old that you have to rethink your entire business?

Well, I'd seen this before, at A. H. Robins back in the seventies, and I knew that when business conditions change, you'd better re-examine your basic premises or face an ever-declining market share. And loss of market share results in a declining stock price. Which in turn causes unhappiness on the part of your Board of Directors and stockholders. Let this fester long enough and your long-term survival as CEO becomes problematical.

Furthermore, the accelerated pace of change in the computer industry meant that the trends I saw would occur faster than those in the Pharmaceutical industry of fifteen years earlier. Software and services companies of the mid-to-late eighties were much smaller than Robins had been and the profit margins far lower. Any decline in sales would lead not only to a decline in profitability, but to an existential crisis. And with no assets to speak of and no cash to pay for the necessary Research and Development, a company might go belly-up almost before its management became aware that the enterprise was in trouble.

CHAPTER FOUR

COMPANY CULTURE BECOMES A FACTOR

So, in spite of the early resistance to my proposals, I felt confident that events would prove me right. Already, there were signs of an industry-wide slowdown. Already, managers were beginning to look at their businesses anew. The success I expected was just around the corner: I was sure of it.

But acceptance of my ideas didn't happen. Not then. Not ever. Why? I wondered. Prospective employers seemed to understand what I was saying. Some even warmed up to me personally. And yet I never came away from an interview feeling particularly optimistic. There was always a curious distance at the close, a sense of coolness.

Now, you might ask, why was I trying to be an employee rather than an entrepreneur? It must seem to a lot of you that I would want to build an empire on my own. Well, it's a question of credibility and money. It is necessary to prove a principle before you can expect to acquire the venture capital to build your own enterprise. And my business plan was especially complex, requiring a front-end investment far greater than I could ever hope to afford. As for possible business partners, say, former consulting colleagues, they were committed to the business model they had grown up with. Independence was not an alternative. Once I was successful with one enterprise, only then I could go out on my own.

I have never been the world's greatest bush-beating salesman. Naturally, the obvious question arose. Was it me? Or did the problem lie with my audience? The more I thought about it–and as the stack of rejection letters, failed interviews and my discouragement grew, I thought about it a lot–the more I began to suspect that something was going on that was in conflict with my reasonable sounding proposals. Something in the psychology of my prospective employers and in me.

That this might be happening made no sense at first–or perhaps I didn't want it to make sense, since I, too, was being driven by my needs. Wasn't the computer business the most rational, least emotional industry there ever was? Wasn't cold logic at the core of all business decisions.

I could understand why someone would reject me personally (no I couldn't, but that wasn't the point, was it?). And yet it was not me but my business case that seemed to turn them off. How could my well thought-out and comprehensive pitch fall on deaf – no not deaf, but fearful and tremulous ears?

I suppose it was hopelessly naïve of me to expect my audience to be so perfectly logical, but isn't there a natural tendency to regard our superiors as being qualitatively different from ourselves? And to be sorely disappointed when they are not? And besides I had such a need for someone to buy into my proposal, who could blame me for shielding myself from the reality of things? Most CEOs are ordinary people no more prescient than the rest of us.

But I should have known that failure was inevitable, my gut was screaming at me.

I realized that I didn't understand people as well as I thought. My intuitive analytical method of reasoning worked only so long as I remained at the level of surface values and constructed personality. When, however, a problem penetrated into the psychic essence of a person, I was entering a region where my own repressed emotions prevented me from understanding what an open heart would have grasped immediately.

But even had I been open to the truths my gut was telling me, I would not have been able to explain them. For I was now dealing with the underlying rhythms of life that are often inaccessible to direct analysis. One must have a unique process of reasoning that isolates the deeper needs of people and explains it if one is to make sense of the bits and pieces of the truth that emerge, seemingly unconnected to the matter at hand. It was not until I took up writing that I learned such a process. And not until the construction of this book that it all began to cohere.

I had never been able to accept as true anything I could not explain yet I had to. In the weeks and months ahead, I kept right on concentrating until I came to the same conclusion that my intuition had known all along: that it wasn't a reasoned and logical argument that was blocking my message, but something far more intransigent.

It turns out that the change I was proposing was unsettling in a way that struck at the very marrow of what was, after all, a very young industry. Having never taken (or had) the time to understand the roots of their success and never seen their industry take any form but the one it now possessed, computer executives were uncertain about their ability to manage change, even well-conceived change. (New systems have sometimes gutted large, successful non-computer companies; imagine the potential devastation of a radical change on a company whose only product is a system).

What's more, the kind of personality that was then a computer executive was unusually resistant to new ideas of management (as opposed to technical innovation). Left-brained people – the logical sort that populate the computer industry – are often paradoxically intuitive, because they have difficulty reasoning inductively. They would rather tinker with reality than think things through. The world of the concrete and the here-and-now, they seem to think, is the only world that exists. It is impossible to foretell the future. Strategic planning is an empty mental exercise.

But there are elements of life which are not conducive to tinkering, the entire sphere of human activity for one. This you deal with, if you are left-brained, using rules of thumb, recent history, conventional wisdom. And the conventional wisdom in the computer industry of the mid-eighties was an unspoken, sometimes only partially understood, conviction on the part of the entrepreneurs and managers that there was an inevitable logic to the way firms in the industry were organized, particularly their business. The structure they had already could not be changed.

Now, structural change in any business is profoundly unsettling. It disturbs the company culture, its personality, if you will. Organizational culture is one of the themes of this work and a complicated one at that. I don't want to devote the space here for a full discussion of it. Nevertheless, a couple of observations now might help to clarify my dilemma in being an agent for change.

Just as an individual's personality leads her to success or failure, so does a company's culture define it. Similarly, the corporate culture that leads to success in one context may lead to failure in another. In the mid-to-late eighties I watched Digital Equipment Corporation, long the principle player in the mini-computer business, struggle mightily to transform itself with only limited success. It failed to save itself because it tried to effect change with existing management and by extension of ideas similar to those that built the company.

A company's culture is formed principally (but not solely) by the character of its founders – and usually the strongest personality among them, If, for example, the principal founder is an authoritarian, paranoid sort, then the people he selects are likely to be obsequious and toadying. The slyly subservient type that is buoyed up by this kind of organization is inclined to be authoritarian with his subordinates – and so on down the line. Similarly, if an entrepreneur is highly creative and likes to surround himself with other creative people, his company may feature an enlightened chaos which may appear (and might actually be) disorganized. The best organization, I believe, looks like a military unit run by an inspired leader, that is, it possesses strong fundamental direction with plenty of latitude for individual initiative.

It's true that many other factors play into the formation of a company personality. Venture capitalists sometimes require important organizational changes as the price of their investment (it is not unheard of for a VC to demand the replacement of a company's CEO). Unanticipated market demand may fundamentally change the approach to business and the relationship among the original employees. The psychological makeup of the rank and file employees often dictates the way they can be managed. For example, while management consultants value appearance and structure, computer engineers are repelled by the trappings of hierarchy. And there will inevitably be skills that the founders of a business do not possess and that must be acquired before it can be started. A software company founded by programmers must often hire salesmen and accountants. And these new skills introduce new personality types.

The values of the community in which the company has its headquarters (imagine the same company being founded in Pittsburgh, San Jose, or Starkville, Mississippi) affect its culture. The availability of specialized talent nearby may influence its prospects. Even historical events in the era of a company's foundation affect the character of the company. A high-tech company founded in the sixties is a very different animal from one created during the Clinton administration.

Yet, despite the sometimes-significant influence of such extraneous factors, it is still the character of the founders that most often determines a company culture. A company's personality is, therefore, formed at the very beginning of its life and tends to permeate and influence the company right through to its demise.

And might, when the company begins to mature, actually *cause* its demise. For when a company is young, almost any management style can be successful, given competent people, the right products and reasonable financial controls. But as a company grows larger, that same style may, like a bad gene that lies in wait for years before it presents itself, cause it to wither and die.

Often, however, a company reaches a point at which it is very clear that its personality is inhibiting its growth. If its leadership is at all perceptive, it will attempt to change things. But this may now be very difficult, since, as the company has assumed shape and become institutionalized, a kind of corporate psychology has also formed, a psychology which is more difficult to change, because it may not map with the disposition of any one person in the business (all organizations are composed of different kinds of people who must work together in spite of their often-conflicting personalities). The company has become the culture it has adopted, much as an adult is the character he has formed as he grows up.

Case in point:

I worked for the A.H. Robins Company for thirteen years, during its glory days and later its slow death during the Dalkon Shield fiasco. During the stewardship of E. Clairborne Robins, Sr., the real founder of the company which began as an apothecary shop on the wrong side of Broad Street in Richmond, Virginia, the company grew, slowly at first then rapidly after World War II. Most of its products could be classified as "remedies" since they mainly alleviated symptoms rather than directly treating the disease. The Robitussin family of cough and cold products was an important brand, Dimetapp Extentabs its profit engine. During this era, the company hired mostly graduates of the University of Richmond, from which Mr. Robins had graduated. Some of them still populated the top management ranks when I joined the company in the late 1960s. In the forties and fifties, Richmond College was a Baptist and mainly day school, populated by young men who were way to close to their mothers. It didn't resemble the academic powerhouse it has become in recent years.

Nevertheless, the company was easy to run and with several blockbuster products, set to grow astronomically regardless of the quality of the staff, who were at least competent in their roles if unimaginative. Mr. Robins himself was fond of rules of thumb and eternal truths (no concept is eternal; one must challenge every preconception). Most of his rules were helpful to him in managing the company.

Then, in the early 1960s growth slowed and Mr. Robins needed to find new ways to justify its very high price to earnings ratio. First, he sold off a large chunk of his own stock to create a war chest for acquisition of products and other companies. Then, at the advice of his public relations manager, he began to hire a "classier" group of middle managers in order to present the sophisticated image he believed was required for national exposure. The people he chose were mainly old Virginia aristocrats, perhaps the most truly conservative class of men in the entire country. Not racist, mind you, but fundamentally resistant to change. There's joke about their kind of conservatism, to wit, "How many Richmonders does it take to change a light bulb. Five. One to change the bulb and four to reminisce on how much better the old one worked." In this era, the back-slapping country club type was preferred.

Mr.Robins insisted that the head of the Research Division must be an M.D., a good practice during the early days of the Pharmaceutical industry. Although not so effective later on, when the M.D. Vice-President of Research experimented with organization after organization which left the research scientists confused and unproductive. During the fifties and sixties Big Pharma was beginning to emerge, and life-saving drugs, such as forms of L-Dopa for Parkinson's Disease, the Salk-Sabin polio cures, and more sophisticated antibiotics, were being developed. Since the Research Division seemed unable to produce such blockbuster drugs, the company would heretofore grow by acquisition.

At first, money was spent on consumer products acquisitions, Polk Miller Products, which sold pet remedies under the Sergeants brand, the Morton Manufacturing Company, whose most viable product was ChapStick, Swinson, a potato chip and cracker vending machine company, and Parfums Caron. Thus, Robins became a mini-conglomerate with marginally profitable, poorly-managed small businesses.

Next and most disastrously, Robins began acquiring drug-related products. Apparently, nobody at Robins understood the phrase "due diligence." Because two of the products acquired led to two of the biggest product liability suits in our nation's history, the Dalkon Shield IUD and phenfluramine, a nonamphetamine diet drug. The Dalkon Shield was acquired so that the company could get into the surgical supply business. No one thought of the inherent risk that an IUD presented, planted as it was inside a woman, and thus given to hidden problems that suddenly manifested themselves. It would have been far better if Robins had acquired a small surgical supply house. As for "phen-phen" as it came to be called, someone should have known that the mountain of paper work required by the Food and Drug Administration prior to approval suggested unaffordable problems.

Many still believe that the reason for Robins' ultimate financial collapse was bad luck. I think I have made a case for the company culture, seeded from the very beginning, being the culprit. That derived from a founder who was a brilliant businessman in a different era, but who failed to manage changing times. Or look for really brilliant people to run his organization rather than those wedded to supposed "eternal verities."

oOo

Not that a change in character is impossible for a company any more than it is for a human being. While the basic elements of a business's psychology are determined early and tend to become fixed, less rigid personality traits can and often are modified as the business adds new employees, enters new territories, engages in new activities or abandons old ones.

The formation of a company personality is arguably as complex a process as the formation of an individual human consciousness. A business is, after all a kind of organism with a life that is different from the sum of its parts. No one (or dozen) personality is best suited to all kinds of business; no one (or dozen) is necessary to the success of any one business.

This is the main reason why it is so difficult to predict that new enterprise will make a profit, no matter how well thought out is its business plan; no matter how competent is the management team. As difficult to predict, in fact, as it is to determine whether or not a given eight-year-old has the stuff (and luck) to rise to the top when he grows up. And the longer the period of time against which success is measured, the more difficult it is to predict who the winners will be.

Not, however, that it is impossible to determine the most likely course leading to success. My whole pitch depended on it. Experience, a knowledge of history, an attention to social and cultural factors, close attention to existing business practices and to the business plan, can lead you in the right direction, the direction of educated guesses and understood risks.

And yet retrospectively it is always easy to see why one business prospered and another failed. For all the possible events that might have occurred, only some actually did occur. And these now seem inevitable and predetermined. And because we attribute the success of a business to these historical events that might have been otherwise, the reasons for these events take on the quality of laws. Thus, in a kind of grand circularity the character of a business is evaluated against the laws its own history created.

Such a way of viewing reality, although hopelessly naïve, comes from the desire in all human beings that there be fixed points, absolute truth, invariable and scientific laws. And nowhere is this longing for predictability and order more poignant than in human affairs – paradoxically because they are the hardest to forecast. And nowhere is this longing for scientific certainty, though rarely coupled with a scientific method, any greater than in the computer industry.

Thus, the successful computer company executive almost invariably concludes that his success was driven by iron laws of inevitably. His own character led to his achievement and his own character will assure that his success will go on forever.

This view of reality, though hopelessly oversimplified, is not entirely a lie. Take E. Claireborne Robins, for example. As regards the company's past success, it was the unvarnished truth.

The trouble with this perception is that most business executives stop with the past. The only part of reality they perceive is the fact that their strategies have indeed worked and that they are, therefore, worthy. Until, of course, there is some difficulty, failure being the godfather of self-analysis. But they rarely want to change the basic organization and the culture and people that got them there. Instead, they try to make do with the organization they've got, hoping their people will respond to the little tweaks they presume will make the difference. They never seem to understand that the future is discrete and not continuous with the past.

The founder of a business rarely questions its past success so long as it continues, believing that it happened as a result of the character of the business that he gave it, a character which is reflected in the strategy and organizational structure which has evolved. And since the business' success, once achieved, seems as permanent as his own success, the strategy and organizational structure of a company must never be changed in any significant way. Only tinkered with as it grows larger and more complex.

The premise here is, of course, arrant nonsense. If conditions and the character of the entrepreneurial management team, had differed ever-so-slightly from the ones actually encountered, the personality of the company would also have been different and maybe radically so. Nor was the business strategy the founder(s) selected the only one available. There were paths not chosen that would have led to success just as surely as the one actually taken. And which may have resulted in a very different business.

During my years as a management consultant, I managed projects in a large number of companies and institutions. And because consultants tend to work in the same industry, I often worked on projects for the direct competitors of previous clients. More often than not these competitors, each successful in their own way, exhibited radically different organizational styles. How could this have happened if organizational dynamics had been so rigidly determined as computer industry executives, my current audience, seemed to believe?

My consulting clients were usually large, established companies outside the computer industry. Nevertheless, the sense of organizational permanence was no different from the high-tech businesses I was now trying to persuade.

Thus, although I would have been a fool to articulate all the implications of a company's culture on my proposals, I understood the principles well enough so that I could at least argue that resisting my ideas on the grounds of the inevitability of the current organization and business strategy was absurd. And I had no difficulty responding to these kinds of objections when they were raised.

And yet…and yet, no matter how hard I tried, my pitch invariably fell on deaf ears. Why?

Because the organizational argument I was responding to was only the surface expression of a much deeper feeling of which my audience may or may not have been aware. For if you are a manager who has never looked at the inner structure of your business critically, but accepted it as a given, then you are unlikely to change anything lest you abandon something essential to your continued prosperity. Thus, while an argument such as mine might seem to be conceptually valid and you may in theory agree to it, it was also subtle. There was no evidence that my ideas would actually work in your situation. And, therefore, you remained skeptical of it.

Your existing organization is, on the other hand, tangible. And to the concrete and linear-thinking mind tangibility equates to reality and reality to inevitability. This is what "hard-minded" really means. As long as things are going well (and even if things are not going particularly well and you can still think of ways to tinker with them), why change?

And it was this intellectual insularity, this inability to see beyond the dynamics of a company or the industry in which it resided, that restricted the already limited vision of computer company executives to the point of blindness. They had help, of course. Although my focus has been on executives who heard my pitch, the rank and file supported and reinforced both the culture and the sense of its necessity.

Here I want to emphasize, in case there is any confusion, what I have already stated, that the audience for my proposals were applications software companies, independent consulting organizations, and equipment companies that had specialized software or specialized talent. Digital Equipment Corporation is an excellent example. It dominated the academic computer market, and had thereby acquired a loyalty among the most highly skilled technicians in the industry. This loyalty paid off for these technicians, so much so that they were able to sell their talents for very high billing rates.

Imagine bundling them into projects led by highly skilled project managers.

Insularity contributes to a rigidity of outlook in two ways. It adds to the impression of inevitability of a company's business practices by limiting a company's view to a very small sample, namely, the company and its direct competitors. And since people generally feel more comfortable being a member of a small group than a large one (large industry groups add to complexity and to too many diverse ideas), insularity, or intentional reduction of the size of your universe, is one of the principal means by which individual employees feel secure. And when you feel secure, you have become complacent.

oOo

Insularity is an inevitable consequence of the maturity of any industry (such as the one that supported IBM mainframe technology) which has grown up quickly and achieved a kind of stasis. The people who manage the industry today are often the same as the ones who began it; they remember the early chaos and are afraid that change might bring it back.

It's not that the beginning stages of a new industry are an experience akin to the Thirty Years War; in a way they are exhilarating. There is a wild variety in the forms of businesses as they experiment with methods of organization and means of product delivery. Everyone has interesting ideas; the universe of potential customers is boundless; everybody is a potential business partner. The world is full of possibilities; a company can be anything. It reminds me of the chaotic development of life in the early Cambrian period.

As a result of this wild and often irrational experimentation, there is also much failure. Trends go nowhere. Hot technologies fail for seemingly unfathomable reasons. But none of this matters much; the stakes are very low. If you are a garage shop operation and the business goes under, the worst consequence is that you might have to move to another garage. The biggest loser is often the unwary investor. I have known people who have founded five businesses before they were thirty, with only the fifth one making any kind of splash.

Then there are the spectacular successes. A company might have the right idea at the right time and its founder or founders become multi-millionaires overnight. In the 1980s most of these successful companies were valued at a few million; the best of them grew close to their maximum size in ten-fifteen-twenty years.

The Cambrian era of wild experimentation cannot go on forever; an industry must define itself or perish. As the industry matures, the businesses begin to grow larger in size, acquiring assets that must be managed and employees who must be supervised. New business opportunities are fewer in number and more difficult to identify. The industry itself is more complex. The stakes are much higher. Protecting what you have becomes a full-time job. The risks of change seem unaffordable.

The eponymous inventor of the Hayes smart modem, which allowed the translation of the products of one word processing system to those of another, quickly built a twenty-thirty million dollar a year business. One of his business partners sold out at the top and became a multi-millionaire. Hayes stayed with the company all the way down to nothing. He even became unemployable because shortly after the end of his mini-empire he went blind.

Insularity is reinforced by salesmen who increasingly call on a certain type of customer, the one he has decided is most likely to buy the product that was built to be simpatico with the idea and culture of the customer. This becomes a much smaller group over time. Internal employees work mainly with each other or with customer representatives that are also like them. In many cases, employees are recruited from customers or competitors. In time, most of the employees have never held a job outside their industry segment.

In the Computer Aided (engineering) Design software, salesmen call on engineering managers and are usually engineers themselves. Trainers and consultants work only with engineers. Executives go to engineering conferences. Sometimes every employee of the business, other than those that service the back office and clerical functions, is an engineer, by training at least.

Eventually this inward-turning begins to define the way the company thinks about itself. Constrained within its limited universe, the company's psychology becomes closed, manifesting itself in a set of commonly held beliefs as to the purpose and function of the enterprise and the necessity of its organizational relationships. This leads to a clannish protectiveness which is adopted by all companies in the industry. This becomes an "industry" personality which may in time become so idiosyncratic that it is likely to astonish a visitor from the outside. A bank branch manager, for example, is likely to feel as out of place in a semi-conductor plant, as a fashion model at a tractor pull.

This sense of shared and inevitable values creates a feeling of solidity and permanence, a comforting sense of the company as an institution, and the illusion of stability. All of which fosters the camaraderie which rank and file employees find so necessary to their own feeling of well-being.

It also leads to a dangerous ossification of business practices. In shutting itself off from influences outside its industry segment, the company lacks the criteria to reexamine itself even if it possessed the will.

Increasingly efficiency comes to lie in hiring people with personalities which are not only appropriate to the job they are performing but fit well with those of other employees in the enterprise. And not in the sense that they like each other or that conflict does not exist, but that they share a common perception that each should exist as a part of the business. If the skills or job title of a new employee places her outside the "necessary" group, she may find herself forced out of the company, regardless of her competence or contribution. Even the commitment of management would not be enough to save her because without the cooperation of her peers, she becomes useless.

A business run like this (and most computer companies were) comes to be managed by a consensus that is more cultural than logical. When there is a conflict between the nature of the job and the employee's talents, it is frequently the job that is changed to fit the employee, rather than the other way around. This is why rationalizing job descriptions or organizational relationships can sometimes lead to an internal revolution; and why new systems can often be ineffective regardless of their theoretical improvement to operations. And, most important to me, why changing a company culture to fit new business realities can be devastating.

How unsettling I already knew, having been an employee of A. H. Robins during its decline and fall while it searched for new organizational structures to make the business grow. Also Digital Equipment Corporation as it tried to use employees already on board to make decisions about things they knew nothing of. And during my years as a consultant. I had personally observed the struggles of companies both large and small to reinvent themselves.

I had already decided that I had better devise a means to minimize the discomfiting potential of my ideas. (Note that once again I had understood the surface implications of my problem – my intuitive analytical method got me that far – without comprehending the deeper consequences). And I reasoned that the changes I was proposing need not alter the company or displace the people that had built it. Instead, I would create a new parallel business using only those existing employees who wanted to join my team. And only then as there were projects to which they could be assigned.

It's true I expected the old business to gradually shrink away – I felt that this was inevitable anyway – but I figured there would eventually be plenty of room for all employees in the new, larger enterprise I helped create. And once the new business began to grow, I felt certain that virtually every employee would want to share in its success and join my team.

As to the senior management of the business that would hire me – why sure it would, if I had my way, have to change some of its basic notions as to the mission and strategy of the company. But an entrepreneur wants to survive and prosper more than anything in the world, doesn't he? If I could get him to understand what I proposed to do, surely this would override his need to preserve his worldview intact.

In this belief I was dead wrong.

CHAPTER FIVE

THE EARLY COMPUTER INDUSTRY

I interrupt the flow of my narrative in order to provide a brief discussion about the early computer industry and how it came to be the way I found it in the 1980s.

In histories of computing there is almost always a reference to the precursors of the modern stored program digital computer. These are interesting but have little to do with the emergence of the computer industry in the 1950s and 1960s.

Instead, we begin with the modern computer as it emerged from World War II under the leadership of J. Presper Eckert and John Mauchly, two scientists involved in the wartime computer project. They developed a machine which they called Univac, the World War II prototype having been called the Eniac, the patent for which the two sold to Remington Rand.

The first true computing machines were not sold until 1951. At the time experts in the field prognosticated that only a half-dozen machines would be required worldwide, the machines being so powerful that only the most outré of applications could use them.

The early Univacs featured a gigantic console, Uniservos or magnetic tape-handling equipment, and a large memory box which used vacuum tubes as short-term storage. I remember seeing a Univac II humming away as late as 1967 in the Kansas City Department of Agriculture office.

While I was there, I saw what happened when a vacuum tube failed or when preventative maintenance was required. The machine was completely shut down so that it could cool enough to allow a technician to walk inside the processing unit, unscrew the defective vacuum tube, and screw in its replacement.

There were other ways early Univac computers differed from later versions. Early computers used manual switches to enter data, but these were quickly replaced as the principal input-output method by punched cards. Rather than the iron encoded mylar tape featured in later tape drives, the early Uniservos used thin iron strips up to several hundred feet long as permanent storage. Once mylar tapes became standard, they were identical to the tape units on stereo systems.

This is where the International Business Machines Company (IBM) comes in. IBM had long been the technical leader in all kinds of business machines. This included typewriters, the most famous of which was the IBM Selectric with its rotating ball which rarely if ever jammed. In the 1960s and 1970s you found Selectrics everywhere save for a few old fashioned manual typewriters, which were inexpensive and thus popular for use by college students and professional writers. Selectrics and most other electric typewriters were too bulky and expensive for casual use. Plus they were not particularly portable. They were very useful in offices with static, immoveable work stations. With the IBM 370 computers in the early 1970s, for example, Selectrics were attached to the console so that a record could be kept of major computer activities, very useful if a program failed owing to operator error or systems failure.

In the 1950s IBM was dominant in card-handling equipment, most prominently the tabulator, a machine which could read cards, calculate and print a business report. These were often attached to collators which could merge decks of cards and also punch cards with the results of computer calculations. There was also the ubiquitous sorter, the earliest piece of large-scale office equipment. Sorters could not only arrange cards, but in doing so could provide counts. The very first sorter was invented to reduce the time it took to take a census to a few months, prior censuses having taken years to complete.

IBM office equipment of the 1940s and 1950s was large and bulky and not very attractive but it could be "programmed" to handle a number of important business tasks. It did this through the use of wires of varying lengths connecting holes representing functions on huge plug boards. The functions these machines could perform were limited, however. There were only so many that could fit on a board. Further, tabulators were notoriously labor-intensive to "program. The wires were very hard to plug in and could be a couple of feet long making a typical plug board into a nest of snakes. Frequently, the technicians would finish a complicated board with bloody fingers. No one wanted to have to go through this again once the board had been wired and checked out. Thus, each individual task had its own set of boards. A big shop had hundreds of them and dozens of machines, sometimes several to complete a single process.

Another feature of these machines was the use of pin-feed forms for printing. These were not the eight by ten forms still found in small businesses such as hardware or auto parts shops. These forms were the size of a king size pillow slip and had as many as six duplicates, each copy being interspersed with carbon paper. The individual sets were held together by perforations, which had to be stripped away to be distributed to end users. They came in boxes big enough to house a small piece of industrial equipment. Once the computer had done with the reports, there were three extra steps before the printed forms were ready for distribution: stripping the edges off of the forms, removing the carbons (called decollating), and separating the still continuous sets into individual sheets (bursting). Decollating was a particularly dirty business because it was at that time when the carbons were disposed of.

The reason I have spent so much space in writing about an obsolete technology is that there are some major implications for later computing. First, the basic printer technology remained the standard well into the 1980s. In the computer age, however, printers became stand-alone devices and became much faster, up to 1200 lines per minute or more (much slower than the compute power in the 360 and later machines). Printing was, in fact, very cumbersome as late as the early Personal Computers and slowed the adoption of

PCs as a piece of consumer electronics. My first PC featured a pin-feed printer the size of a typewriter and twice the weight. It produced copy that was unusable for formal correspondence. The whole system had a footprint the size of an elephant's.

Since many systems were designed around punched cards well into the 1970s, card sorters were found in almost any shop of some size. And most data centers had keypunches for data entry. A really big data center such as the one in which I worked in Philadelphia in 1965-66 might have forty keypunches running two-and-a-half shifts a day. With card "chaff", the stripped edges and carbons for printed forms, and boxes of forms and cards either completed or lined up for processing, data centers were very messy and noisy places.

A third implication of the unit record (another term for card) era was the low status of even the most experienced programmer (called a project planner) of card-handling equipment. It was considered and paid as a clerical job slightly below an Accounts Receivable clerk. When the first digital computers were introduced, many of the unit record operators became computer operators and project planners became programmers. As a consequence, many early computer programs had a strong resemblance to the features and functions of their plug-board predecessors. With only three or four hundred lines of code, a program might be and usually was replaced every year or so. In this way the programs became increasingly rich in function and sophistication.

Because IBM was dominant in the card-handling market, it was natural that it would become a force in the business computer market. Company managements were rarely computer literate and didn't want to be. It was a status symbol *not* to have a machine on your desk. Managements were perfectly willing for internal data center employees to control early systems. And in IBM shops, IBM was god to computer staffs.

Because the predictions for computer use were limited, only very large organizations with a single "killer" application chose to afford one, Univac became the standard nomenclature for all computers. Simultaneously, IBM began to reach the apex of its annual sales for card-handling equipment. As a result, Thomas Watson, Senior sold off a part of the company.

Univac, too, saw business computers as, at best, a support for card-handling equipment. They also believed they had the patent for the idea of a computer, a perception which eventually merged into a Federal antitrust suit against IBM which, as I have said, went on for many years. Univac believed that their biggest computer business opportunity lay in carving into IBM's unit record market share. To force customers to make the right decision when converting from unit record equipment to computers, the only input method the early Univac computers permitted was their proprietary Powers card.

Even people in their eighties have probably never seen a Powers card. This is because it never secured even the smallest part of the computer market. I saw Powers card-handling equipment only once, in a Federal data entry office in Chicago. The office was situated in a dusty three-story walkup on the bad part of South Side. It was so antiquated that the sorter had clawed feet like bath tubs of the 1920s.

The Powers card was about the same size as IBM's Hollerith card, but was divided into horizontal halves and thus could support up to ninety characters of data, forty-five characters in the top half and forty-five at the bottom. In this it resembled the ninety-six column cards IBM introduced many years later for the System 3 computer. The System 3 card was much was much smaller than either the Hollerith or Powers card, however, and was frequently used where businesses wanted compactness. These computers used BASIC, a simplified language often used in academic computing, as their computer language which made it incompatible with all of IBM's other systems, a real liability in building a networked capability later on.

Because of the very unique Extended Binary Coded Decimal required for the Powers card it was much more difficult to design a keypunch and other card handling equipment then the much more straightforward IBM card.

The Hollerith/IBM card was designed by Herman Hollerith to work with early card-handling equipment. His company was acquired by IBM in the early part of the twentieth century when the only device available other than a keypunch was a sorter. For the young majority who have never seen card data entry, the Hollerith card featured eighty columns, each having rows for 0-9, the selected number being punched. For alphabetic entry columns were double-punched. It was this format of card that was used in the disputed Florida voting for President in 2000.

One of the advantages of the Hollerith card is that numeric entry is straightforward and numbers represented probably 90% of the data entered. The actual character keyed was printed at the top of the card. This made it easy to "patch" cards with tiny strips of tape if erroneous information were entered or programs needed to be changed. This proved a boon to programmers who could change their programs through patching rather than being forced to wrestle with data center priorities to get a reassembly (an assembly is the process by which programmer language was translated into machine language).

On the other hand, the Powers card with sometimes multiple punches in each column was much more difficult to patch. Until the System 3 in the 1970s all IBM equipment used the Hollerith card. This included all early computers. As customers gradually converted from unit record equipment to computers, they didn't want to flush their investment in keypunches and existing unit record equipment until the replacement computer programs were ready. Thus, IBM had a leg up on competition right out of the gate.

As it turned out, Univac did not have exclusive rights to the idea of the computer or at least couldn't get federal judges to rule in their favor. By the time the antitrust suit reached the Supreme Court, IBM was considered a national treasure, with technology that far outstripped its competitors and many, many vendors that used or were attached to IBM machines.

One lesson that the industry learned from the Hollerith vs. Powers experience was that if you own the *de facto* standard, you own the technology.

Not that there weren't other attempts to improve on data entry. Teletypewriter coding was useful for long-distance data transmission. Some computers used punched paper tape. Magnetic strip cards used mylar tape on large cardboard cards, principally to maintain customer information and history. Magnetic strip cards were also used to write and store programs,

Another reason IBM became dominant in the computer market was the invention of business computing. Early on, all computer applications were big number-crunching jobs developed primarily in scientific laboratories. This is called scientific computing and remained a minor factor in computing until just recently. IBM was willing to play in this market and did, although only half-heartedly.

The much bigger market lay in selling computers to businesses to replace traditional unit record applications such as Payroll, Accounts Receivable, Order Entry, etc. Customers were able to improve the applications and simplify clerical procedures. Oddly, many of these traditional applications were not cost-effective when run on a computer, mainly due to the cost of the machine, specially prepared data centers, and programming. But a company that did not convert its applications was one that was less progressive than its competitors.

In spite of the upfront cost, IBM needed to convince enough customers to buy the machines so that they could be mass produced and generate the huge profits that resulted.

oOo

Even the smallest first or second-generation computer was a massive beast that would occupy the better part of a room. Because the machines required extensive cabling, they were usually placed in rooms with a raised floor underneath which the cabling would be run. This may seem to be a huge disadvantage to computerizing, because it involved an additional, not insignificant, capital investment for an already expensive conversion. Many companies made this an advantage, however, by locating computer centers in special rooms with large plate glass windows on at least one wall. These were covered with curtains which could be dramatically opened to show special guests the magic machines actually working!

Computers became a showcase for a company's progress. In television programs such as the early Mannix, a data center was usually shown with a flat-topped man ripping some huge piece of wisdom off the console printer and then rushing off to solve the world's problems.

Because nobody outside information processing professionals had any idea what was really going on (or wanted to), it all seemed so futuristic and magical that every company of any size had to have one. And the bigger (in physical size) the machine the better.

IBM was very early to recognize the Hollywood glitz driving the data center. It didn't hurt that all IBM equipment was painted in a restful light blue that immediately drew attention. The front panel of a 360 featured a large number of blinking lights that had no other purpose than to look pretty.

Univac, still trying to sell mainly scientific computers, was left in the dust.

The entire computer industry was faced with a problem that significantly slowed its growth. In the late 1950s and well into the 1960s the industry suffered from a severe lack of programmers and systems analysts. Computer programming was a brand new, rather complex, skill that had never before existed. Nothing remotely like it.

As we have seen, many computer departments retrained unit record operators and project planners to be programmers and systems analysts. IBM strongly encouraged this, claiming programming was a skill quickly learned.

It soon became obvious that most unit record technicians lacked either the logical intelligence or the attention to detail or the imagination to fill either of these capacities. Most wound up being computer operators, a far less demanding job than programming. Besides, the pool of tabulator technicians was considerably smaller than the need for programmers.

Still wedded to the idea that programming was easy, some companies promoted clerks to fill the jobs. Since many clerks were college-educated women underemployed by the Culture, a large number of them were successful as programmers. I suspect that there has never been a time that so many women held down well-paying jobs in the computer industry than in the beginning. Of course, promotion was well-nigh impossible, but this was the era when women in general became more visible and assertive in the work force, the bare beginnings of the women's movement. And programmers made a lot more money than nurses or educators.

But where were all the people needed to *train* all these technicians. College was not a good source. There were very few Computer Science programs then and these tended to take an engineering track. There was no such thing as a Business Information Systems major, either. Some junior colleges, especially in California, tried to take up the slack, but instructors could make much more money practicing the trade instead of teaching and soon departed the groves of academe.

That left IBM itself to do the training, which is where I learned my first computer language. But these courses were aimed at turning out programmers fast, ready or not. Reminds me of the old engineer joke, "Six months ago I didn't even know how to spell ingineer and now I air one." Only with programmers it was more like six weeks.

With the failure of so many of the early programmers and the lack of qualified applicants, almost any reasonably intelligent person could enter the field. Hell, they even hired English majors like me.

Gradually a critical mass of technically-oriented people came to be employed. Few were particularly imaginative and many early computer applications resembled the old manual or semi-automated systems. Most systems were big report generators.

Worse, the early systems were hampered by lack of computer capacity. The first computer I worked with was a sixteen-kilocharacter IBM 1401. The 1401 was a second-generation computer using magnetic cores as working storage rather than vacuum tubes (thus the term "core dump" still used today for full memory print-outs). Each core represented one bit and was either turned on (a one) or off (a zero) in a classic binary structure. These bits were interconnected with wires which performed the on/off under command of the Central Processing Unit. Machines with core memory were much more efficient and less subject to failure than those with vacuum tubes. Second generation computers were still very large, however. The 16k machine I operated required four large boxes stretching half the width of a data center.

Several other companies joined IBM and Univac as competitors in the industry. Most were giant industrial firms with a background in electronics, including GE, RCA, and Westinghouse. Usually late to the game, they obtained so little market share that the industry came to be referred to as "IBM and the seven dwarfs".

IBM didn't neglect scientific computing entirely. It commanded a large percentage of the market for super expensive, high performance computers. In the second-generation era, it built the 7000 series computers, most especially the 7090 which was the most powerful system extant. In the mid-1960s I operated an IBM 7074 at the Defense Personnel Support Center in Philadelphia. It differed from the 1401 in that its internal coding used 40-character words. This allowed for ten numeric characters or five alphabetic/special characters. A word-oriented machine performs calculations many times as fast and much more precisely than the 1401, because arithmetic operations were performed in parallel rather than a character at a time, usually in index registers specially designed for calculations. The 1401, by contrast, performed calculations in memory. This made an application requiring several divides, say, pathetically slow.

Another feature of IBM 7000-series computers was high-performance magnetic disks. Although disk drive capacity was minuscule in comparison with modern day computers, the physical units were extremely large. One disk surface was nearly as tall as a human adult. Magnetic disks were giant boxes with three electromechanical read-write arms. These moved quickly to the spot where the data was stored, similar to moving a record-player needle from one track to another. The trouble with these early units was, being mechanical, they were subject to periodic failure. Sometimes you might lose one or even two arms in a single night. Then you were forced to run in a degraded state. I remember several nights when, covered with sweat, waiting for work that should have been finished at two or three AM still running at seven. There was one weekend that all three arms went down almost simultaneously. And we're talking about the era of the Vietnam War buildup when volumes at the DPSC were going through the roof. We were days recovering from that snafu.

The problem with running a mixed technology shop as we had then was that the 7000 series and the 1401 were two radically different architectures with two different standards. This was resolved in the next generation with the introduction of 360 architecture which featured four-byte words and sixteen index registers. Each byte permitted two numeric characters or one alphabetic/special character. In this way it was similar to the 7000 series but each byte was also a discrete unit as in the 1401 series.

The 360 series allowed programmers to run 1401 programs in 1401 emulation mode. This allowed users to gradually transfer older programs to the new machines.

Which brings us to the final, and, probably most important, IBM-owned standard in the early days. Early programming languages were machine specific. The programming language in the IBM 1401 era was named Autocoder; in the 360 era it was called Assembler. A program written for an IBM computer could not run on any other machine...and vice versa.

In the late 1960s there was a national movement toward standardization to assist in converting one vendor's technology to another's. Thus was introduced a more English-language programming language, COBOL, or COmmon Business Oriented Language. In the 1401 and even in the smaller 360 computers, COBOL was a memory-hog and very inefficient to run. Later on, as machine capacities swelled and internal speeds grew much faster, IBM bowed to the demand and introduced its own version of COBOL, COBOL Level D. IBM's COBOL could not run on any other machine, however, effectively thwarting the standards objective.

In the next chapter we will see more implications of proprietary standards on the industry and its psychology.

CHAPTER SIX

IBM'S ABSOLUTE DOMINANCE OVER THE COMPUTER INDUSTRY

I was wrong about the impact of my convictions on my executive audience because my proposals challenged a couple of beliefs that formed the bedrock on which the software and services industry was built. First was the belief that if a computer business executive were to upgrade the quality of services his company provided, it could be done by the people he already had. These were most often the sort of people who knew IBM technology and the software or consulting sold by his own firm (that insularity again). And, second, that IBM was too large and powerful a company not to be able to respond successfully to any issue.

I was, of course, well aware that my proposals challenged the conventional wisdom (I had actually counted on a little skepticism, otherwise, I would be telling my audience something they already knew and where was the value in that). And nowhere were my ideas so radically challenging as in the notion that Big Blue (IBM's company logo was printed in large light-blue block letters) was not the invulnerable monolith that industry insiders perceived it to be. What I understood far less well –at least until that dark night in 1988 – was the power of the image IBM had created for itself.

By 1985 IBM had been the dominant force in the computer industry for over thirty years, the entire working careers of virtually everyone then employed in the industry. And although this dominance had been achieved through marketing clout as much as the quality of its product line, it was no less real for all that.

The principal means by which IBM had established and maintained this dominance was through control of its customer base. IBM had made it oh, so easy for a company to adopt its platform of the moment ("platform" is the name for the complete hardware and software "package" delivered with the computer) as the basis for its computer effort. And, oh, so difficult for a customer to go elsewhere once it was committed to IBM.

As we have seen in the previous chapter, the main method by which IBM had accomplished this industry control was through its use of numerous proprietary standards, software and/or hardware products owned by it but which became *de facto* industry standards.

Now, the power of proprietary standards should be familiar to anyone who owns a Personal Computer, Microsoft's Windows operating system being a well-known example. A company with a proprietary standard can, for example, prevent anyone else from using it without its approval. It alone decides what its products will become; it alone determines the pace of progress within its industry. Features can be incorporated into a proprietary product that make it difficult for a competitor to build an auxiliary product (such as a security system) as "integrated" as its own. This allows a company to dominate areas of an industry undreamed of when the original standard was created.

The result is a kind of monopoly, but one that is very different from the brute force domination of a Carnegie or a Rockefeller. For such a monopoly depends neither on control of the means of production nor of the channels of distribution, but on the ownership of intellectual property. Nor is this ownership like a patent on a drug since similar drugs with small improvements or different formulations often pop up overnight. If a company were to introduce a better computer or at least one that functioned just as well as IBM's equivalent, the customer would still be locked in because conversions would be prohibitively difficult (I'll discuss this shortly).

Even the computer hardware is a kind of intellectual property. Its potential for obsolescence means that virtually all its value is contained in its engineering design. The owner of a proprietary standard need not own any physical assets.

And yet such a monopoly is more coercive than the oil and steel trusts of a hundred years ago. This is because a proprietary standard uses the free enterprise system against itself.

American business is built on the premise that the creator of intellectual property owns it (thus, copyright laws). But what if that property is a software "package" and not a book? What if that package is the only one that can be used for a particular type of business problem? The package is now a standard and ownership of that standard gives its owner absolute power over it use.

Of course, applications software does not follow these rules because most such companies are quite small and the advance of technology in general often makes an older software product obsolete. In the early days of Personal Computers there were several Word Processing systems, Wordperfect, Wordstar, etc. Imagine running a small business without a Personal Computer word processor (except in the beginning when there were stand-alone word processing machines).

Vendors of systems software, that is, software built into the operating system and into which other software products are integrated are another matter. Search engines for the Internet, for example. This is how Word, a late entry into the word processing world or Excel, similarly late as a spreadsheet, became the standard. They were both owned by Microsoft and were initially bundled with its operating system.

But who says this product is the standard? What Czar of industry has ordered it to be used by all?

Here's where the subtlety comes in. Nobody has said it, it has just happened. And nobody actually restrains competition. No one prevented anyone from writing an operating system to compete with Microsoft. But no one did (except for IBM's OS, an abject failure). Why?

To understand you must examine the unique characteristics of the computer industry.

The main reason for proprietary content in any product is to make it appear different from (and thus presumably superior to) its competition. In this, a computer is no different from a box of soap powder. But while Gain works just the same as every other laundry detergent (in principal, anyway) and is normally used for doing the laundry only, an IBM AS/400 does not work like any other computer and has almost unlimited uses. This flexibility makes the modern digital computer very complex to operate (I bet most of you know this from your PC experience where some types of software just don't work the way you think it does, requiring much trial and error).

Early on, computer manufacturers saw this as an opportunity for themselves. If a manufacturer could imbed software and hardware features which would make its systems not only different from but incompatible with his competitors, he could make it impossible for a customer to move applications to someone else's platform without a costly – and often highly risky conversion. Given this unpalatable option, most customers would choose to upgrade their existing technology rather than convert. This is why customers, once they were committed to, say, a Burroughs system tended to remain with Burroughs through all succeeding generations of computer technology. In this way computer manufacturers could effectively *own* their customer bases.

One might note here that a conversion from platform to platform became much more difficult as time went on. This occurred because most business and many scientific computers ran multiple applications with sometimes thousands of programs.

In the early days virtually all programs were custom developed by internal computer departments. Functional sophistication was limited by available tools and the rather unimaginative staffs of the era. As staffs began to change and become better educated, programs with more features began to replace the original versions. Unfortunately, the systems development methodologies remained unchanged. Typically, this involved little more than shooting the breeze around a table, then programming a little, shooting the breeze a little more, programming a little more. It was a process that might go on for weeks or even months. This produced what was referred to as "spaghetti code" all tangled up with itself and hard to follow. New programmers inheriting these programs often had a steep learning curve just to figure out which parts of the program actually did something and which ones were obsolete. Whereas the very earliest computer applications might be completely replaced every six months or a year, the more complex new systems had to last for years, often with new code heaped upon old. Eventually many of the bet-your-business applications became a permanent part of the business repertoire for as much as 20-30 years. You can imagine how frightening was the prospect of having to replace one of these unwieldy monsters.

What if a manufacturer of a computer company owned not just a competitive percentage of the available customers, but three-fourths of the entire computer market as IBM did? What would be the effect of proprietary standards then?

Well, *any* new product such a company introduced would automatically be given first preference by all its customers. This would be true even for those products not all that aligned to its original standard. In the 1970s, for example, many customers adopted IMS as its data base management system, not because it was the best available or the most efficient or the official industry standard but because it was IBM's offering.

For any competing product to gain acceptance, it would have to be clearly superior. This was hard to prove since it is only through considerable use that a customer can be sure that a software product works as he hoped it will. And even though it might perform acceptably, it will never exactly meet expectations since computer programs are mechanical objects, perfect according to their own lights, though impossible to completely explain with all the manuals in the world.

Thus, a new IBM product, by default, was almost always acquired by more computer users than its competition. And this advantage only grew over time, since developers of software products, much less concerned about computer limitations, and wanting the largest market possible, would build their products around IBM systems. *Their* customers would also be forced to buy IBM systems. Soon customers, who in the beginning had chosen a competitor, would find themselves forced to convert to the IBM product. This would eventually lead to IBM-based software systems becoming the industry standard, which would automatically make systems developed for other platforms, non-standard.

oOo

A company as shrewdly managed as IBM was bound to exploit this kind of market power to the fullest. By the late 1960s IBM had created several proprietary standards. The most important turned out to be 360 architecture. For the first time in IBM's history, the late 1960s era 360 computer featured an operating system. There were actually two not entirely compatible operating system platforms. OS, which was directed at its very largest computers, and DOS, more limited in its capability and aimed at medium-sized users. OS formed the core of IBM's mainframe technology from the time it was first introduced, although it went by many other names, OS/MFT, OS/MVT, MVS, etc. OS became the foundation on which all later IBM mainframe software products were constructed. Some, like CICS, the online transaction processing manager, and IMS, the data base management system, themselves became *de facto* standards.

The reason the 360 platform was one of the most important single innovations in the history of computing was that for the first time software became more important than big iron. While it is relatively easy to copy hardware (and there were companies that did make 370 add-ons), it is much less easy to copy software, especially systems software. Once you own an operating system your developers will find it relatively easy to add new features, while a competitor must first decipher the operating system code before they can proceed. A new version of the operating system required extensive testing and any features of your programs that were non-standard would have to be converted. Even a conversion from DOS to OS affected every program in a company's repertoire, often taking years to complete and was fraught with risk. A company in Richmond, VA developed a product to make DOS look more like OS, but it was always subject to blocking software and achieved a very small market share.

IBM's near monopoly over the industry had the predictable chilling effect on competition. Any new computer user who chose a competitor instead of IBM risked condemning his company to life out of the mainstream. And any existing customer foolish enough to try to replace an IBM system with "Brand X" would not only find his software options limited but would also be forced into a costly and time-consuming conversion. And vice versa. As a result, the smaller manufacturers found themselves reduced to niche markets.

oOo

IBM's domination of the rapidly expanding computer industry made Big Blue the darling of Wall Street. With nearly absolute control of its customer base, IBM could regulate its pace of expansion by managing the pace of technology. It was commented at the time that choosing IBM was like growing mushrooms, "you keep them in the dark, feed them s—t and they will grow slowly." It's true, however, that IBM introduced quality, even innovative, products in its first thirty years in the business.

Since any computer's capacity is fixed and the thirst for new or improved applications unquenchable, IBM could be sure of making a new sale to almost every customer at predictable intervals. And since technical needs advanced much more rapidly than machine capacities, the new machine would cost much more than its predecessor even when the new machine's enhanced performance would easily cover the price increase. The exponential growth in the need for computer capacity was driven by four processor-eating technologies – remote entry of programs, on-line data entry, data base management systems, and a new generation of third-party applications software. This seemed to guarantee Big Blue an ever-growing revenue stream.

IBM controlled its growth in profitability also. IBM could charge its customers a premium for its products while introducing new versions at a pace that maximized the sales for any older version. It could, for example, milk the demand for one generation of computer before introducing the next. This encouraged IBM to inhibit technological progress (and made it a little complacent, too), but who cared so long as the business prospered. Compare the slow pace of the growth in computing in the IBM era with the doubling of processor speeds every year-and-a-half over the last twenty years or so.

Not that IBM could ignore the drive for continued improvement in its products. The ability to sell more and more powerful machines depended on IBM's being perceived as a technical as well as a marketing leader. The competition, even though weak, was still making advances. So-called minicomputers were beginning to appear on the scene and very large super computers were increasing the size of that niche. Control Data Corporation and later Cray became the dominant players in this market.

Since the markets for both minicomputers and supercomputers remained comparatively small, IBM could easily ignore them, As time went on minicomputers became increasingly powerful and supported many new applications. To compete against minicomputers, Big Blue introduced a line of small business computers (System 3, Systems 34, 36, 38, AS/400, et.al.) that were quite successful. But they were incompatible with IBM's mainframes, using RPG as the language of choice and a completely different and incompatible technical base. IBM called their small business computers minicomputers but they bore no resemblance to the real minicomputers sold by the Digital Equipment Corporation, Data General, Wang, etc.

Still, when a new IBM product was not all that innovative, it was almost always a real enhancement to IBM's product line. Since the pace of technological change remained far in advance of the capability to make use of it, IBM's customers were by-and-large satisfied with whatever new features IBM offered.

The appearance and often reality of IBM's technical leadership allowed it to market itself as something more than a conventional profit-driven enterprise. Many industry pundits believed that Big Blue's dominance of the industry was all that perpetuated America's leadership in computer technology. I once heard Dick Brandon, an early industry guru, refer to IBM as a "national treasure". Others asserted that IBM's huge size alone allowed the U.S. to compete with Japan, Inc.

It should be no surprise, therefore, that the technicians who filled the rapidly expanding internal computer departments often viewed IBM as a transcendent institution like a nation or a church. Because these technicians were for the most part untraditional sorts, isolated temperamentally and socially from their peers in, say, accounting or marketing, they had little sense of affiliation with their employer. Their principal loyalty was vested in a profession whose standards were set by IBM.

Technicians were not, therefore, reluctant to use the power of their arcane and yet necessary knowledge to intimidate their managements in their own professional interest. For their part, corporate managements were, oh, so willing to allow themselves to be intimidated. Unwilling to wrestle with the confusing and alien details of computer technology (it was too mechanical, I suppose, like assembly line work), most managements found it easier to delegate the complete responsibility for vital corporate systems to internal computer departments. This led to these departments becoming a third force within corporate America (stockholders and management being the other two) bent on enhancing their empires in the name of efficiency, which almost always meant an IBM solution.

It didn't matter that computer applications were not always cost-effective or that end users frequently hated their computer applications because they were balky and difficult to work with. IBM was never selling operational improvement anyway. What it *was* pushing was the appearance of technical sophistication – and technical complexity was one way to achieve that end. Which was yet another reason why programmers and operators loved IBM – complexity added to the mystique of their own skills made them seem more valuable and their pay grew accordingly. A complicated system was usually one that was costly to run, requiring more and bigger computers, which did nothing to diminish IBM's revenue growth, either.

○○○

All of this was, of course, marketing, the most sophisticated and subtle marketing system ever devised. I have only begun to suggest its intricacy.

And yet it was also elegant in the simplicity of its principles, its linchpin being those proprietary standards again. These, increasingly with time, were not just those of the central computer or its operating system, but of every product where IBM could set a standard. Thus, while the main goal of every new IBM product introduction may have been an improvement to the technical capabilities of its total systems, it was rarely the motivation behind the specific implementation chosen. The real objective was the establishment of a new *de facto* standard.

One way we know this for sure is because IBM's product was always different from and incompatible with the equivalent offering of its competitors even where an industry standard existed and might have been used.

The hunger to own every standard is the reason why IBM worked so hard to neutralize open standards such as the COBOL computer language. And why IBM always proposed a bigger, better, but always radically different, whizbang, whenever a new technology reared its head. Examples include a hierarchical data base management system, IMS, rather than the networked standard; binary synchronous data communication rather than asynchronous; broadband networks rather than baseband.

○○○

One area of computing that IBM never tried to dominate was applications software. We can only speculate why this was so, but the fact that the software industry was emerging simultaneously with the U.S. antitrust suit against IBM must have been an important factor.

The inherently fragmented nature of the computer software industry, which made it unattractive for a monolith like IBM to participate, must also have contributed.

The reason for IBM failing to dominate the computer consulting industry is much clearer. As a consequence of the settlement of the antitrust suit, IBM was forced to divest itself of the Service Bureau Corporation, its consulting arm. This allowed the emergence of very large, sophisticated competitors such as Arthur Anderson (now Accenture) and Ross Perot's EDS. And since computer services are a peculiarly personal business with many, many possible skills, very small, specialized entities also found a niche. The lack of IBM participation in this industry did not imply lack of IBM control, however.

Very few software companies were willing to risk designing applications for non-IBM systems without also possessing a better IBM equivalent. Those that did were regarded as outlaws, designing third-world applications for third-world companies. Even though a few software firms sold versions of their IBM-based products that also ran on competitive computers and some services firms hired technicians that knew non-IBM software products, the mixed vendor consulting firm was rare.

There were several reasons why this was so. The most obvious being that by selling to IBM customers you had far more of them to whom you could sell and when you are a small company you want to go after the main chance.

On the other hand, you also had a lot more competitors. That IBM customers represented a very large market was not lost on anyone entering the software business. Nobody was preventing you from developing products for multiple platforms, especially since being a big factor in a small market might be just as profitable as being only one of the competitors in a large one.

This strategy was rare because the more vendors you support, the more different skills you have to possess. And there are only two ways to obtain those skills: either by cross-training existing employees or hiring new ones.

Clearly, cross-training was not an option. An IBM literate technician would have to engage in costly and time-consuming retraining to become competent in another platform. In doing so, he would have risked the eventual obsolescence of his IBM skills. This, if he was any good at all, was something he was not about to do.

The other alternative of hiring non-IBM skills meant adding new types of employees and buying additional hardware and software to develop the new product in a business that was already over-specialized. Unless you had grown big enough to manage that kind of complexity, you didn't even want to try.

An even bigger obstacle to the multi-vendor shop was the inevitable culture clash between the IBM staff and the non-IBM newcomers. Non-IBM technicians tended to be independent freethinkers, unconventional in appearance, introverted, uncommunicative and hard to keep on track. If these were their only attributes, management could probably live with them. What a multi-vendor company will find intolerable, however, is that the non-IBMers generally hated IBM and did everything they could to debunk IBM products and standards. This immediately placed them at odds with the IBM loyalists who loved the very idea of IBM and saw the non-IBM crew as too unconventional and incompetent to boot. And unless you kept these two groups physically separate, the resulting in-fighting could tear a company apart.

Besides, IBM offered incentives to their more successful vendors, incentives that were usually not available to companies that also supported their competitors.

Note that proprietary standards tend to polarize people into ideological camps, proprietary versus open standards, for much the same reason as religion polarizes orthodox believers and heretics. In every human heart there is a tension between respect for authority and resentment at being controlled. If one is to resolve this tension, one must decide which is the greater evil totalitarianism or anarchy, and come down mainly on one side or another. If you don't you are always conflicted. The lover of proprietary standards, of IBM, wants to believe that there are eternal verities and absolute standards of dress, ethics, manners, etc., while the devotee of industry standards prefers openness and democracy. The two groups inevitably hate each other because they have had to reject the alternative in themselves.

oOo

Another reason non-IBM software vendors were so rare was that there were comparatively few available entrepreneurs who knew non-IBM technologies. Since software and services entrepreneurs grew up in an industry dominated by IBM, they were much more likely to have experience with IBM products. Many of them had been IBM-based technicians at one time or another (do you get the impression that the noose is growing tighter) and those that had not been IBM technicians had at least grown to understand IBM's unique brand of technology and felt comfortable with it. Examples of the latter were persons who had been trained in a university on, say, a Digital Equipment Corporation computer. In the IBM world, more than a few entrepreneurs were former IBM employees, often salesmen or systems engineers.

These executives naturally admired IBM as a company and tended to emulate its unique culture in their own businesses, often regarding themselves as beneficiaries of the world IBM had built. And for all their own wealth and power, they often saw themselves as creatures of it – any orthodox believer derives his personal authority from its theoretical source – God, IBM, you name it. Very much like Spain in the era of the Inquisition.

This, of course, further encouraged the insularity of these companies, an insularity which was of no little advantage to IBM's domination of the industry since it closed off the possibility of heterodoxy.

oOo

Insularity, blind loyalty, emotional commitment to a concept, all powerful weapons in IBM's control of the computer industry. But they all depended on one factor: IBM's continued dominance of the technical as well as the business side of the industry. If IBM were to stumble, if the notion of its invulnerability were shaken and if a few IBM loyalist companies were dragged down by that failure, then the psychological underpinnings of IBM's control might be destroyed.

IBM was not about to let a stumble occur in its core business computer market. Unwilling to rely on its huge size, financial clout or command over industry psychology, IBM engaged in certain business practices which further discouraged competition. One weapon was IBM's relationships with senior management of large corporations as supported by a professional image among its employees, an image that gave off the aura of impermeability. I will discuss this aspect a couple of chapters later.

It had always been bandied about in the industry that IBM severely punished those individuals and organizations that strayed from the IBM standard, but this could not be proved; such overt actions would have been illegal. What was certain was that Big Blue rewarded its loyalists. Sales leads, technical assistance, even investment money might flow to the IBM-compliant company (not to speak of the prestige of being an "IBM reseller" or an "IBM preferred vendor," not so different from the "Intel inside" label on PCs). Better assistance went to the most compliant vendors.

There is nothing unethical about any of this; a company has every right to reward its friends. But in an industry as fragmented as the one for software and services, IBM's activities had a profoundly coercive effect.

As late as the mid-1980s few software companies had a monopoly over even such a restricted market as the one for Payroll. As a consequence, most IBM-related software and services companies remained quite small. A large service provider might employee 1,000 persons and generate $100 million in sales. Software firms were smaller still. The support of IBM and its giant sales force was often all that lay between a business and its extinction.

Thus, even in the face of technical weaknesses which were beginning to manifest themselves, IBM was able to maintain its dominant position.

One effect of IBM's marketing panache was that my proposals were much more difficult to sell than I had first expected. Not that the IBM-related company executives were unaware of the new technologies that were beginning to raise their heads and that IBM had no immediate answer for. Nor were they resistant to changes in business practices *per se*. So long as my ideas were hard-shelled technical in nature, then my audience was very willing to buy into them. What they could less easily accept was the abandonment of the idea of Big Blue that filled their imaginations.

I had been a manager in an IBM-based computer department for ten years and was well aware of the ways that Big Blue could manipulate its power to maintain its market share. How it often used its clout to discredit any suggestion that it might not be as all-competent as it wanted you to believe. (I am not paranoid about this. IBM did not drive me out of the industry. It didn't have to. I was never more than a mosquito flattened on its windshield).

I was convinced that there is a logic to the direction of technology that cannot be denied forever and that IBM was, therefore, in real trouble and I tried to convince my audience of this.

I know this sounds like delusional megalomania on my part. Worse, it seems self-destructive. Why would I throw myself on my sword by spending so much of my time in front of business executives harping on IBM's weaknesses which would soon become apparent, when my proposals didn't depend on it and my other arguments were just as powerful? Truth to tell, there was my anger at my status in life, which came out of deeper psychological needs of which I was then unaware.

And then there was the more obvious fact that I started all this in 1985 when I was a Big Six Consulting Manager looking around for a hook on which to hang my practice and the first thing that came to mind was the radical change in my perception of Big Blue. All the thirteen years at A.H. Robins had led me to believe that IBM was an unassailable force and now that I had been given broader responsibilities, I began to challenge that belief. My organizational and management ideas came later and only gradually. It was year or two before this observation led to the idea of the "solution sale" as I perceived it to be.

Further, my argument became much stronger should companies be forced away from pure IBM technology. Companies finding themselves in this fix would have a massive conversion ahead of them, one that would require much technical assistance that they did not have inhouse.

And, finally, there was my conviction that I was right. Companies that depended on IBM would be dragged down if they didn't form a plan to cope with the inevitable decline in Big Blue's fortune. It would help my credibility enormously if I could convince a prospective employer of this. And, besides, if I didn't have some such story to tell, some immediate and pressing reason for a change of the magnitude I proposed, why would they change at all? I had to find a way to penetrate the insularity of their thinking.

CHAPTER SEVEN

HOW IBM'S CULTURE INFLUENCED ITS MARKET DOMINANCE

By the mid to late 1980s the computer industry had changed in a fundamental way. And IBM's business structure – and its mainframe base – had not and, maybe, could not adapt to these realities. And yet nobody seemed to know it.

Maybe a few people. Or nobody would have competed in the rapidly growing segments of the industry as the Compaqs and Digitals and Suns were beginning to. But nobody in the space in which I had spent my career, namely, business information systems. IBM still had that market sewn up.

And yet I was convinced that IBM was also vulnerable here. How could this be?

It seemed that the changes in the industry were not just changes in technology, but was a response to changes in the way corporations of all types were being organized. This new cultural organization was a reflection of a change in values of the larger society, which were very different from the values and structures of postwar businesses.

It was this older social organization that IBM's culture affirmed. IBM's internal culture and external image were unusually pervasive, even systematized. Its implications penetrated into the very marrow of IBM's collective being. Without it IBM would no longer be IBM. Not in the perception of its public and surely not in the minds of its employees. It was so deeply ingrained that it permeated all the way to IBM's approach to technology. Why the very concept of a mainframe computer was a reflection of it.

It was also a powerful marketing tool, since it affected the way the company worked with its customers. It maintained an image which was the ultimate in MBA-type professionalism and extraordinary hierarchical at the same time. The latter was thought of as a good thing in the 1950s since it facilitated top-down communication and made sure that there was a consistent view of technology and markets throughout.

To change that approach to business was to reverse what modern business practices seemed to imply. A whole embattled world view would be put at risk and that would profoundly shake the computer industry – and more generally, the corporate social contract in all businesses.

oOo

To begin to explain the roots of IBM's decline, therefore, we must first look at its company culture. And to understand its culture one need look no further than a feature of IBM's marketing system which I have not yet discussed, a feature fundamental to IBM's historic growth, and integral to IBM's culture, namely, the IBM image.

The IBM image was pervasive everywhere you encountered the company. In the severe and understated yet assertive logo. In the colorless and boring marketing materials. In the squared off yet sensuous design of the equipment (the front panel of a fifty-year old IBM 370 still has value as a showpiece). In the dense and unadorned technical manuals. In the orderly and impersonal office space.

But most of all in the business "uniform" and rules of conduct of its representatives.

This image was a surface presentation, yes, and had no direct relationship to the quality of the products. But its implications on the business world were much more than skin deep (appearance always is, you know). It was no less than a tangible representation of what IBM aspired to be. In this it was almost sacramental ("an outward and visible representation of an inward and spiritual grace"). The IBM image had been carefully constructed by its founder to be a representation of the elite status of its representatives, both marketing and technical. It had been improved upon and institutionalized over the years to reflect the unique position of Big Blue within American culture.

To the world at large IBM represented orderliness, competence, unfailingly functional products, prompt and professional service, financial stability, and to its stockholders the expectation of infinite growth. That this was also how America in the forties through the early sixties perceived itself to be and what America believed excellence looked like arose out of the necessary logic of the postwar period. In that era IBM was the apotheosis of Capitalism in its most developed form, even more so than Peter Drucker's idea of General Motors in *Concept of the Corporation*. In the Manichean world of the Cold War this kind of Capitalism was viewed as the only bulwark against the serfdom represented by the U.S.S.R.

Although curiously it was not the Capitalism of untrammeled competition that was our one defense against the Reds. Rather it was the Capitalism of the giant, quasi-monopolistic enterprises. As if large corporations, and especially IBM, were not without a kind of totalitarianism of their own. It was a totalitarianism so obvious that Apple's famous *1984* Super Bowl ad was able to parody IBM as the image of faceless and soul-deadening anonymity without referring to Big Blue by name.

On the other side was the myth of Communism perpetrated by its supporters. According to them, Communism had found the secret to rapid industrial growth, which lay in massing its workers into immense industrial complexes and coercing them into greater and greater productivity. During the postwar era many actually believed that Communism would actually win (which was why McCarthyism reared its ugly head and the paranoia of a nuclear apocalypse led our country in many very silly directions). Against the relentless onslaught of this brutal juggernaut, the only way America could maintain its competitive edge was by marshaling our considerable organizational skills. More than anything else a hierarchical and highly structured organization was the secret to our victory in World War II and our ability to avoid returning to the Depression after.

America had no taste for the national planning and state enterprises that were restoring Europe. Instead, we put our trust in a few giant corporations. And it seemed the only way these enterprises could be managed was through scientific management, another World War II discovery. Industrial engineering, compartmentalization and specialization of both white collar and blue collar work, and, increasingly, computer applications.

As the principal manufacturer of the tools that formed the backbone by which systemization was possible, IBM was both the sponsor of the institutional corporation and its best example. With its reservoir of both human and financial resources, it offered both stability and order to its industry, a Pax IBMica.

By contrast, the high-tech booms and busts over the last twenty or so years have been deeply unsettling in their unpredictability.

The computer world of the IBM era seemed to permit growth without risk. This image of imperial imperviousness as much as its proprietary technology allowed Big Blue to be seen as a national resource.

The IBM image was both the external representation of the preternatural efficiency the new industrial organization seemed to imply and a comforting symbol that, after a decade and a half of depression and war, we were a society in control.

(A curious and unknown fact is that Stalin was opposed to the very idea of the computer for various ideological reasons. His intransigence on this matter permitted the U.S. a lead in computer technology it has never relinquished, contributing in no small way to the declining competitiveness of Soviet industry and especially to the backwardness of Soviet missile guidance systems. The Cold War may have been won and lost owing to this technological gap. And the Space race surely was).

Depending on their rank within the company, IBM had many rules its employees were to follow that controlled aspects of their lives. The neighborhood in which the employee lived was one of them. A Branch Manager was supposed to live in a much posher community than a sales manager, for example. A sales manager lived in a more upscale neighborhood than a salesman and so on down the line. An employee must never live better than his supervisor even if he had private means. This held true for the make and model of the car he drove, the status of the clubs he might belong to, etc., which implied a hierarchy of taste. These rules were spelled out down to local specifics. They imposed a uniformity of social and political values. In addition, promoted IBMers could never remain in offices in which they had held a lower rank. This dictated frequent transfers to minimize the envy of one's former peers. Unfortunately, this also replaced the psychic connection to kith and kin and sacrificed many long-term friendships as well

The dress code was a major element of the individual's image, reinforcing the impression of machine-like efficiency. It was commonly believed that in order to be systematic you must also be orderly and nowhere was orderliness and status more clearly reflected than in a man's personal appearance. (Woman were almost never a part of the field staff then).

It was not neatness alone that IBM demanded. "Clothes make the man," it was often said. A subdued and expensive mode of dress confirmed an elite status, an image that IBM wanted its sales representatives to convey. Though not too aristocratic a style of dress; that was reserved for the upper echelon. IBM wanted to portray its people as belonging to an elite of accomplishment, a meritocracy. Also, a representative must be clean-shaven and until the late 1960s wear a hat. It helped if you were six feet tall or better, not too ethnic-looking, well-groomed and Nordic.

In an era of "casual Fridays" and cut-off jeans and tennis-shoed dot-com companies, this emphasis on surface presentation must seem quaint. But in the context of the American value system as late as the 1970s this emphasis on personal appearance reflected a reasonable perception of a man's value. Democracy was perceived as a system that allowed the most able individual to rise to the top.

The kind of institution worthy of a man's loyalty was one where the path to the top was well defined. When the path to the top is ill-defined, the criteria for success are subjective and subjectivity encourages selection by whim. Further, a professional appearance implies malleability and malleability a willingness to conform to a system. Without the system the whole organization collapses. Thus, appearance seemed a reasonable criteria for selection and advancement.

It can be inferred from all this that most jobs back then were intellectually undemanding and required little creativity. The system rewarded people who could perform mundane tasks very well. Too much imagination was often a liability and stimulated resentment on the part of those who don't have it, especially when it comes to wending your way through a giant corporate bureaucracy. Of course, such a system is monumentally totalitarian – and slowed the growth of the company IBM needed to become.

Then there was the role the IBM image system played in maintaining IBM's market share.

IBM's image was, to emphasize a point, a reflection of its company culture, which like all cultures, reflected the collective values of the members who survived and prospered. What was revolutionary about this particular culture was not that Big Blue's people reinforced these rather stifling values and did not have to be compelled to follow them, but that these were institutionally defined values and not derived from the informal organization as most company cultures had emerged.

The dress code was the most visible of IBM's conformist measures and illustrative of the subtle effect the system had in managing its employees. For a dress code is really a uniform and the wearing of a uniform implies commitment to a set of principles for which the uniform is a tangible symbol. The uniform of a beverage company route salesman, for example, suggests he belongs to the beverage company and must conform to the systems and ethical values necessary for the beverage company to remain in business.

This kind of uniform and any worn by so-called working class employees confers on its wearer a lower middle class image. This is the reason why employees, as they rise in occupational status, try to escape wearing one.

The principles behind a military uniform are much richer than this. Except for a few furbelows on dress uniforms and the insignia of rank there is little difference in uniform between an officer and an enlisted man. A military uniform is one of the means by which group behavior of a predictable kind is encouraged. (It is interesting that the institutionalized military uniform showed up about the same time as large national armies, in the seventeenth century). In the first couple of centuries after their origin, the design of national military uniforms varied with rank and arm of service. Thus, a dragoon wore a much different uniform from a hussar, and an officer from a private soldier. This suggested the very different social status of the wearer and the very different psychology one must carry into battle (cavalry was much higher in social status and much more disorderly in battle than the "regimented" infantry). The gulf between officers and "other ranks" was so great that the Duke of Wellington referred to the latter as the "scum of the earth."

Later, when armies became prosecutors of national aims, uniforms came to reflect the mass psychology its leaders wished to reinforce. The uniforms of the World War II participants are illustrative of this principle. The German uniform reinforced the insecure Romanticism of the Nazis, the Russian, the beetling conformity of state socialism, the American, the practical utilitarianism of Capitalism, the British, the conservative class consciousness of Tory England. Field uniforms were consistent in design for all its wearers regardless of rank and arm of service (save for the Navy).

The IBM dress code closely resembled the twentieth-century concept of a military uniform. More elegant than ordinary business attire, it suggested that its wearer was in the business world but somewhat above it. It also implied that working with your mind was more aristocratic than working with your hands (IBM's corporate motto THINK was explicit in this way). The farther you got way from the machines IBM sold the higher the status. The sales and management attire were more aristocratic than that of IBM's technical support people, called Systems Engineers (SEs) and the SEs in turn, dressed more formally than the Customer Engineers who maintained the machines. Also like a military officer's uniform, IBM's dress code suggested that the company's sales and management team was a member of an elite legion whose purpose was worth devoting one's life to.

The IBM image was practically as old as the company. It came as a result of the older Thomas Watson's theory as to the way IBM products could best be sold. The IBM image was both a reaction to the environment in which the company found itself and a manipulation of it.

Office machinery, Watson believed, represented an entirely new type of product whose purpose and function were often difficult to explain, but whose use might have repercussions at the highest levels of business. This was true even before computers came along. Typewriters, tabulators, copiers, facsimile machines, calculators, all involved major changes to office procedures. The company most likely to grow a large office machinery business, let alone win a competitive sale, was the one whose marketing organization would best relate to a customer's senior management. This was because only senior management could effect the organizational changes required to implement the new procedures. As late as early business computers the departments that actually used the new equipment were too low on the totem pole to make such decisions. Up until twenty years ago there was no such thing as a Chief Information Officer.

IBM salesmen were encouraged to call on and maintain relationships as high in the customer's company as they could, no lower than the Controller, and sometimes as high as the President, if at all possible.

Calling on a company President was one thing but maintaining a relationship was quite another. The latter required that the salesman be seen as the social peer of the President. In the 1920s, when the IBM culture began, this meant projecting an aristocratic demeanor. A salesman must look upper crust, which in that era meant a starchy, Wall Street, dark suit and white-shirted standard.

In order that this not appear to be a façade only, the entire company must be made to appear to be something special. Offices were maintained in some of the fanciest real estate available with private offices for any person that dealt with the public, elegantly appointed conference rooms and pristine demonstration centers. Everything that would make IBM into an Olympian organization, far above any other company, let alone one in the office machine business.

But why was this necessary when CEOS themselves were frequently crude, rough and aggressively middle-class? Well, everyone aspires to a higher social status and to be approached as an equal by a man with so much polish that he seemed to gleam, especially when accompanied by a mannerly and obsequious bearing, could allow the crudest robber baron to entertain the illusion that he was an aristocrat, too.

Even though lower level IBMers such as Systems Engineers need not and, indeed, could not meet these high standards (SEs were more like to be overweight, never actually obese though, or a woman or, much later, an African-American), but everyone who serviced a customer had to adhere to a reasonably high standard of social skills and appropriate appearance. The result was that IBM presented a "professional" look that was highly admired and widely emulated.

To understand the revolutionary implications of this image, one must remember the widely-held stereotype of the salesman that existed prior to IBM. Back then, salesmen were backslapping Rotarians, slick-talking con men, "drummers", capable of bedding the farmer's daughter and charming a few extra bucks out of an unsuspecting prospect. A carnival barker who was poorly paid and of very low social status, at best a Willie Loman, at worst a Sammy Glick.

The IBM look radically undercut this perception of the salesman type. Well paid and quietly personable, the personal presentation of IBM representative was so much in contrast with the older stereotype that IBMers seemed not like salesmen at all, but above it all, professional and disinterested, aiming at informing the customer not selling him. And since this impression was reinforced by the quiet austerity of practically everything that constituted IBM, the company itself came to be seen as more of an institution than a vessel for profit.

By the 1980s, however, most companies had their own internal office machine specialists and the implications of the complexity of computing had become so foreign to the day-to-day operation of the company, that the manager of a computer department was now an executive within the company. He was almost always college-educated, in many cases with a degree in Computer Science or Business Information Systems. IBM representatives now called on data center managers rather than the corporate senior executives. In many cases, they were prevented from going over the heads of the data center managers. This did not change the perception of IBM as the last word in computing and the ultimate arbiter when it came to the use of systems technology. The relationship between IBM and its customers remained one of advisor-client more often than salesman-customer.

This was always an illusion, however. IBM salesmen were paid mainly on commission, which strongly motivated them to maximize sales even when a new product was not in the customer's best interest. No one seemed to appreciate that the advisor-client illusion was like giving the IBM representative the PIN number to the company's bank account.

The control that the computer department and by extension, IBM, could exercise over a company's business operations was not well understood. Most companies delegated all responsibility for business systems to the computer department, executives at all levels choosing to remain ignorant of their own systems. In turn, the computer executives, knowing just how hard any kind of conversion to a technology other than IBM would be, chose to depend on IBM for everything. If the potential for conflict of interest in all this been commonly known, it would have made no difference. The logic of IBM's mastery of the computer industry would have forced corporate systems in the IBM direction anyway.

One implication of the Big Blue style was that it was a marketing company first, never a high technology company in the way most industry companies are today. Salesmen and management made the big bucks and were promotable all the way to the top. You couldn't become a Branch Manager or higher without having spent time as a rep. The technical people who developed the product were, for the most part, invisible and seen as second-class citizens. Even today when it is comparatively weak, IBM does not operate by the same rules as other high-tech companies and shouldn't be regarded as one.

CHAPTER EIGHT

THE IBM IMAGE COMES IN CONFLICT WITH THE CHANGING SOCIAL PARADIGM

IBM's marketing system was not without great cost, however. Maintaining its image as a disinterested advisor required Big Blue to engage in a lengthy and service-intensive sales process. If a salesman were to maintain his relationship with the customer until the next big computer sale, which might be years away, he had to sustain a constant flow of activity. And it had to be activity that made business sense. Golf junkets, cruises, parties at the Country Club, all had their part to play, but they always had to be tied into some business purpose.

Fortunately, it was not all that difficult to find some reason for sales activity. The technical complexity of computer products, software as well as mainframes, required formal presentations and informal discussions between IBM representatives and internal computer specialists. Software often required demonstrations and discussions of marketing documentation. And there was a constant flow of new product announcements.

IBM carried this pre-sales support well beyond the mere sharing of information. Training sessions were often part of the sales process as were some types of applications design and development activity.

There was also plenty of handholding during the installation of a computer system. And in those instances that IBM did not have a product to meet the customer's need, say, a university fund-accounting system, IBM sales representatives might coordinate the work of third-party vendors, sometimes serving as general contractors in a multi-vendor competitive bid situation.

Since a large customer might be running dozens of applications on hundreds of pieces of equipment using thousands of programs with a computer staff in the hundreds, issues and opportunities that required a sales representative cropped up almost every day. The senior salesman on the account had to react quickly to any pertinent customer activity (let alone any activity on the part of competition in what IBM considered its baliwick), while the Big Blue response frequently required many man-hours, days, months to research and completely reply. So complex would such a customer be that it might require several IBM salespersons.

This level of effort also required large numbers of highly skilled technical resources and of many kinds. No one person could know all there was to know about all the different computerized processes in which the customer was involved—or even some of them. By the 1980s the role of the salesman had changed from a technical advisor to a resource coordinator.

The effect of all this support was, of course, to further lock in IBM's customers to Big Blue's brand of technology. If IBM always had a reasonable and timely answer to any technical question, if IBM products always worked as its representatives claimed they would, if IBM could find the resources in its huge bureaucracy to address every customer inquiry, if Big Blue actually anticipated customer needs, why should a company's staff talk to anybody else? Even though IBMers were, after all, human and the quality of support depended on the kind of person assigned and could sometimes be spotty, customers were convinced that IBM the company was an impervious monolith and would ultimately make its mistakes good.

This was, of course, worlds apart from the sales approach of the minicomputer companies that made hay on scientific computing. They assumed that the customer was competent enough to engage with the technology on his own. But the minicomputer approach was a two-edged sword – without comprehensive support his customer had little reason for brand loyalty.

All this support had not so favorable consequence for IBM, however, namely, the creation of a huge and unwieldy bureaucracy, and, too often, jobs that were suffocatingly boring.

oOo

It has often been said that the worst aspect of a totalitarian bureaucracy is not the oppression, it's the frustration in dealing with all the rules and procedures. It didn't take Fascism for Kafka to imagine the absurdity of *The Castle,* only an administrative job in an insurance company. IBM's egg-to-earth institutional culture and assembly line style of management was totalitarian bureaucracy *par excellence.*

IBM's bureaucracy was made all the larger and more complicated by the vast extent of its reach. In addition to vertical integration of its computer products, IBM still competed in all its traditional office machine markets. It sold typewriters, copiers, old-style electrostatic facsimile machines, business forms, even leases and maintenance contracts on the few pieces of old style tabulator/sorter/collator machines that hung around computer departments for as much as twenty years after they were obsolete.

With many layers of management and staff just to enforce its rules and communicate them to the rank and file and a belief in the technical perfection of its administrative control systems, it's no wonder that Big Blue was by the early 1980s a bloated organization of almost a half a million souls.

oOo

A huge and intermittently responsive bureaucracy can have a devastating effect on company performance, however. The sales force loses interest in anything except personal gain. Administrative people become officious and haphazard. Managers reward adaptability rather than excellence. The entire organization becomes complacent. And jobs become organized to the point of tedium.

Worst of all for IBM was the fact that the most tedious, the most unrewarding positions wound up being those whose incumbents would tolerate it the least, the skilled technician jobs, especially those in the field.

At IBM a good technical consultant sold himself, a bad one was worse than useless and yet the bureaucracy was equally loyal to one and all. When I was a Big Blue customer I rarely encountered a really competent SE. The better ones were usually booked to the hilt by bigger companies that required IBM talent much if not all of the time. Probably because we didn't use them much, our company saw the inferior performer again and again,

Whether they were good or not, in demand or not, all of Big Blue's technicians were dying to move to sales. For its part, IBM was only too willing to let that happen. Sales was, after all, the engine that drove the business, and a technical background might make a new salesman a quick study when it came to the lengthy and complicated sales effort. But not all technical people had the confidence, adaptability, communication skills or personal appearance to be an IBM salesman.

Too often, therefore, the SE on your job was either inexperienced or an ineffective and demoralized timeserver. But you hired them anyway because sometimes it made more sense to buy a marginal talent for a short period of time than to hire a permanent employee and be stuck with him forever. The customer that chose to use an SE had better structure the work so that it was as unchallenging as possible. This left the occasional good SE I encountered underutilized and underappreciated.

In addition to being ruled out of the more lucrative career paths, the talented though not elegant IBM technician was reminded of his lowly status in many ways. Even though it was his skill that actually closed many deals, it was the salesmen that got most of the credit and the financial recognition that went with it. And the technician received no commission for his efforts.

When on top of everything else, the IBM technician was expected to conform to the dress code, although in a slightly less formal way, and all the rules and procedures the IBM image entailed – at a time when the average industry technician looked nothing like the IBM image – an SEs status must have been like rubbing salt into an open wound.

A good rule of thumb is that the more technically competent a person is, the more careless about appearance he tends to be – and that goes double for his social skills. A really brilliant computer engineer is often as marginal a personality as the most outré artiste in Soho. On the other hand, he will be willing to work himself into an early grave with stunning results.

This was the personality that was beginning to emerge as early as the late 1970s, replacing the stereotype of the flat-topped engineer at Mission Control in Houston.

Programmers were a bit more adaptable to strict rules than computer design engineers (they had to be, there were so many of them by then that they were a commodity). But they, too, chafed under the IBM management control systems. The more sophisticated the programming skills, for example developing or maintaining an operating system, the more independent the personality tends to be and the more that they balk against heavy-handed management procedures.

Since a company looking for technical help can do without social graces, but not competence, IBM's customers rarely balked at the heedlessness of externals of their own staffs. IBM itself could not tolerate it, however. What was at stake was not just the appearance of a few technicians, but something much more disturbing, namely, a sea change in value systems in the larger society, a sea change that challenged IBM's management system and the world view that it entailed.

This sea change in mores emerged out of the political and social chaos of the 1960s. It was at bottom a paradigm shift in attitude toward authority. Before the 1960s, existing authority was seen as an inevitable consequence of civilization. Afterwards, it was viewed as an arbitrary thing that might be dispensed with if it proved inconvenient. And not only was the hierarchical authority of managers and subordinates called to task, but also the authority of Western ethical and value systems which went under the name of Christianity or the Enlightenment.

The immediate causes of the paradigm shift in this country were the Civil Rights movement and the opposition to the Vietnam War and what both did to erode faith in constituted authority. No longer would our institutions of government be looked on with unwavering reverence. Even the people that represented the older authority were reviled and sometimes spat upon. This included the military, the police, criminal courts and other bearers of the mantle of authority. The Democratic Party, the titular representative of what was progressive in American politics, experienced rioting during the 1968 Chicago convention.

Student radicalism was not just a phenomenon of the United States. In Europe, Civil Rights and the Vietnam War were of little consequence. Most countries in Europe were run as Social Democracies and Colonialism was mostly a dead letter. Yet Daniel Cohn-Bendit was as influential a presence there as Mario Savio or Jerry Rubin in this country. And the Baader-Meinhoff gang was just as destructive as the Weather Underground.

The real cause of the paradigm shift was much deeper than any transitory movement. It was no less than a repudiation of patriarchical authority under the influence of the increasingly Leftist mass media and the growing radicalism in thought at the progressive universities from which the highly intelligent 1960s radicals graduated, then joined the faculty and gradually wrested control of the Liberal Arts departments. Although 1960s radicalism soon died away and its troops got jobs and raised families and moved to the suburbs, the underlying belief system never completely disappeared.

Professional dress gave way to "casual Fridays" and later "business casual" every day. Liberal politics became the purview of only one party. Hierarchical levels of authority in business gave way to a much flatter, more open management style. And technical people of all races and genders began to make headway against the Nordic totalitarianism. U.S. History was no longer thought of as universally benign and our republican system not necessarily the best form of government in history.

Thus, in spite of the election in 1980 of Ronald Reagan, one of the most reactionary Presidents in modern history, the new paradigm persisted, more muted for a while, but still there. In fact, modern Conservatism would be unthinkable without the paradigm; the Clinton impeachment fiasco would have been unimaginable in the Kennedy administration. By the 1980s the new paradigm had found its way into the board rooms of corporate America and even, with much resistance, into the military (Women Generals? Unthinkable.)

Hegel was right. Social change begins with the expression of an idea in the purest form possible. Toward the end of the 18th century, it was a radical movement that aimed to sweep away the old regime and all its outmoded structures. Then there is a counterrevolution by which conservatives try to restore the ways that have been "lost". This, too, is impossible because the radical movement arose out of a very real social dynamic. In the end the left and right must come together into a new system which preserves as many as possible of the *forms* of the old regime within the logic of the new paradigm.

Thus, while the radical movements of the sixties of the 1960s proposed doing away with constituted authority and the political and social structure that supported it, it quickly became clear that civilized order was impossible without some kind of enforced discipline. The mass of men found the illusion of stability comforting and some kind of authority system essential. But it was clear from at least the Nixon years that the old authority system was no longer viable and that some new system was required.

What might that new paradigm be?

History works by transforming only what is objectionable about the existing order. And what was most objectionable about the older system was that those in command not only exercised control over the functions of their institutions but also tried to impose their values and perceptions on those over which they held sway (*a la* the IBM system). Because authority figures in the postwar era tended to possess simple and conservative values, their systems tended to enforce the way things were.

That had worked in the 1940s and 1950s when America was trying to return to normalcy, and when there was the common perception that American democracy was "A-OK" just the way it was. But as the 1960s progressed, a number of the values and perceptions that had formed the postwar social contract, some that went back to the very establishment of our Republic, seemed morally bankrupt.

Take white supremacy, for example. White supremacy was institutionalized into national law until the 1940s and state law until the 1960s and is a *de facto* fact of life today. And since it was part of the national fabric, sometimes unconsciously so, institutional authority tended to reinforce it. The IBM system clearly favored white Nordics, for example.

White supremacy and its partner, immigration exclusion, goes back to the 1840s with the anti-Catholic Know Nothings. While these primarily southern European immigrants were white and eventually merged into the larger white society, ethnically-based immigration restrictions of one sort or another persisted until the 1960s.

This is not quite the same thing as White Supremacy as currently defined. This was and is an animus towards former slaves, exclusively from Africa and nearly always black, many of whom had been residents of this country for hundreds of years by the time of the Civil War. What we now call African-Americans were visibly different from other persons, although a number were free and lived in free or border states by 1860.

Nevertheless, the general American attitude towards The Other, whether through anti-Hispanic immigration laws or the Asian Exclusion Act or the concentration camps built for Nisei Japanese or the failure to accept European Jewish refugees during World War II was a distinct and related reflection of a national phobia.

Institutionalized White Supremacy was discredited by the Civil Rights movement and so were the business and governmental systems that supported it. But that did not end racial bias or the subtle suppression of disfavored groups. Nevertheless, the 1960s was an era when our society's attitude to the more egregious versions of ethnic prejudice was overturned.

It turned out that the values and perceptions of the existing order were not only corrupt but also inefficient. The invention of the cotton-picking machine made share-cropping obsolete. The notion that bigger is inherently better was disproved by the failure of the conglomerate idea. The notion that women forced to work outside the home should be relegated to helping positions such as nursing, public school teaching and secretarial/clerical unnecessarily reduced the pool of management talent at a time when business success was becoming increasingly difficult to attain.

Changes had to be made.

Now, it is not possible to have a unified civilization without both values and generalized perceptions of the truth. The more structured the civilization, the more obtrusive will be the cultural system that supports it. For example, racial segregation did not really take hold until the South began to become urbanized in the 1880s. The Congressman from Wilmington, North Carolina was black until 1892. Since our nation has become more structured in the last century or so and will continue to be, our institutions have had to reflect that change.

And so the question that beset our civilization had to be rephrased: Given that cultural perceptions are both inevitable and obtrusive, how do we see that the values we create out of the new culture do not impose another aberration like white supremacy?

The solution as proposed by the new paradigm was something like this: First, we must regard the values and perceptions of the traditional culture not as immutable laws but merely cultural norms which can be changed as conditions change. Second, if the new norms are also relative, they are also individual, meaning institutions should enforce theirs only as the institutional mission is affected. And institutional missions should always be narrowly interpreted. A company should not attempt to regulate the sexual behavior of its employees, for example, even when such behavior reflects badly on the business.

And third, since institutional rules and the conditions of work are often intertwined, a business should, as much as possible, avoid imposing its authority on the way the work is performed once the process under which the work is to be done has been defined. This holds especially true when it comes to white collar work, although quality circles have done much to improve assembly line productivity.

This does not mean that the new paradigm opposed collaboration, quite the reverse, the work of the individual should benefit all employees at the same time it accomplishes its mission.

What the new paradigm dislikes is a Boss. Of course, someone must coordinate the efforts of all or chaos results. From Brook Farm forward socialist communes have failed as a result of the tension between community needs and individual desires. The manager need not be an autocrat, however.

Many years ago my computer manager, who was struggling with his own penchant for authoritarianism, asked me how the organization should be run. I told him that each person should have a specific job and should conform to the specifications of that job. A programmer should not, for example, go off in his own direction without authorization. My manager in shock said, "you mean run things like a military unit?" And I replied. Yes, though not like a cadet corps, but a combat unit where everyone must do their job or the mission fails. Where the company commander is willing to accept input from the lowliest Private if the latter knows something the commander does not. Where everyone thinks his job is important and everyone is loyal to the group. Otherwise, the unit will fly apart psychically and wind up being destroyed." Unfortunately, he was a Manichean thinker, inured to thinking it was either one way or the opposite and never got the point.

The objective of the new way of thinking was a new kind of authority, one that was fairer and more democratic, an institutional authority without an institutional dictator. What might this new type of authority look like?

The answer lay in making the enforcer of authority not a man but a system. And not just any system, either. It should be a system capable of being codified objectively. Since rules should never be changed in the middle of the game, also a system that is defined in advance.

But what should this kind of *system* look like?

One alternative was the rule of law translated into business, where there would be a big policy and procedure manual that attempted to define the parameters of individual action within a well-defined job. Of course, any law is subject to manipulation and is thus unfair. Worse, most employees in this kind of system perform only their jobs and do not stray outside it when conditions seem to require interdepartmental cooperation.

Another and still more comprehensive system was the one suggested by the IBM culture. But that was deeply hierarchical and anti-individualistic.

What wound up being implemented in the new paradigm was a system based on a set of rules that defined most routine decisions and yet was consistent and fair in its application. Something derived from scientific theory as exemplified by the works of Peter Drucker and others. This was the MBA approach ruled by formulas and statistics, economics and management theory.

In the eyes of its practitioners the computer itself was this kind of system. A computer operates completely without human bias (it was theorized). Although the program that causes the computer to work is a human creation and a programmer can manipulate it for his own gain or merely his own ego, proper controls on the programmer's work, such as comprehensive testing, can minimize these biases. With other controls, the biases of the system controllers can be minimized – and so on. What could be fairer than that?

The computer did not, however, replace the arbitrary judgments of human managers or eliminate hierarchies. Until very recently, it didn't do anything more sophisticated than automate existing clerical processes. Even when it began to be used to facilitate decision-making through so-called Artificial Intelligence or complex integrated systems that tied together the factory floor, product distribution, and traditional back office systems, no changes in management psychology resulted. Even then humans could devise ways to thwart systems and continue to run things as arbitrarily as they always had. What the new systems did accomplish was to provide a symbolic totem for the new paradigm. The new systems aimed to assure fairness by removing human judgment (and often human relationships) from all processes relating to the rewards and penalties of the workaday world.

It was perceived by computer advocates and the naïve that this goal could be accomplished through a blind and emotionless surrogate such as the computer. From tabulating test results to compiling affirmative action reports to calculating cost of living statistics upon which retirement benefits are derived, our society is unthinkable without the illusion of objectivity that computer programs permit.

And if not the computer itself, by a computer-like process with predefined and inflexible procedures (thus, mandatory sentencing guidelines). No one saw that all this fairness was like IBM totalitarianism on steroids or that no human mind could grasp a comprehensive business solution without letting his personality influence the solution.

The act of computer programming itself was an example of the new paradigm in action. If the program was to be the exemplar of objectivity, then the person writing the program would have to make himself machine-like. The more precise and logical a programmer was, the more effective his end product would be. This gave little rein to imagination in the literary sense.

Each program is an individual effort crafted through a very demanding intellectual process and is as different as the personality that created it. Although a program's features must conform to a predefined set of written specifications, the actual way code is written is often defined by the programmer himself. This makes him almost an independent contractor, only one who happens to work within the comforting walls of an institution.

The craft of programming recalls an earlier America, an older pre-factory artisanship and the Jeffersonian ideal of the yeoman farmer and individual proprietor. But because it happens in context of other programs written by other people, computer programming is a Jeffersonianism of the system. And, as we shall see, the systems view of management that this view encourages is not without baleful consequences.

The new paradigm is thus a result of the development of the more expansive computer age which began in the 1970s. Then why did it take until the mid-1980s for it to begin to have an effect on the structure of the computer industry? Especially considering the fact that such revolutions as "just in time inventory" management were already taking place. Well, first there was the image of IBM as the impervious monolith, which was difficult for an industry executive to see beyond. Second was the difficulty of converting out of the old spaghetti-code world into the new more comprehensive, and cleaner applications.

Also a liability that had to be surmounted were certain historical developments which had to reach maturity before internal departments were forced to change. These included the competition of the Japanese in computer technology (they were the first to develop the dense memory chip), the maturing and coming to power of the Baby Boomers and their very different view of society, and the impact of Personal Computers in forcing computer literacy on previously resistant managers. These factors accelerated the move to high value technology, ideas that were already situated in the hearts and minds of the more progressive technical people.

This eventually led to the diminishing of the absolute control that IBM maintained over the industry and over the imagination of the society at large. With the loosening of IBM's control which very few people could see in the mid-1980s, the forces of the new paradigm were let loose with a vengeance.

CHAPTER NINE

HOW IBM WAS VULNERABLE IN SPITE OF ITS MARKETING CLOUT

In the previous chapters I referred to a sea change in American culture that flew in the face of the IBM's traditional "professional" image. I have gone far afield into the social and philosophical implications of that change to indicate how pervasive was the change and how permanent. That this was apparent to me way back when was a result of my being dragged out of the insular IBM world in the early 1980s and into a job as Big Eight Management Consultant, where the view of the industry was quite a bit broader. And with my drive to understand the consequences of new information, my opinions began to change.

By 1985, three years into my time at Peat Marwick (now KPMG) I had reached the conclusion that IBM's dominance within the computer industry was one of those "laws" that was really a tautology: IBM was a rich and powerful company because it was large and profitable. But since the rules that defined the industry had changed, even reversed, Big Blue was now as vulnerable to business shocks as its smaller competitors. From a company of real technical excellence, it now depended on its marketing system to retain its industry dominance. It did this through manipulating psychology, proprietary standards, control of customers and business partners and outright coercion. All this while the computer industry was increasingly dependent on accelerating technical innovation.

My opinion was not, however, shared by the Wall Street pundits who continued to promote IBM stock even at the unprecedentedly high Price to Earnings ratio at which it then sold. According to the conventional investment analyst, value was achieved in two ways, one by long-term growth in revenue and profitability and the other by marketing presence as exemplified by a constant flow of new products. According to the conventional view it was marketing that made postwar America great and it was marketing that put IBM on top – and would keep it there. Articulate and persuasive management at IBM made the stock analysts believe that IBM was too much on top of things to ever decline. And until the eighties there was plenty of evidence that they were right (although the Wall Street experts have been wrong so often about technology that it makes you wonder why any sane small investor would gamble on high-tech.)

All you had to do is look at the enormous companies that had tried to compete with Big Blue, some much bigger than IBM, and yet none made a dent on the industry. Even the United States Department of Justice had failed to break up IBM in its interminable antitrust suit. IBM had hired former Attorney General Nicholas DeB. Katzenbach as general counsel and quickly ended the suit with a compromise. One of the consequences was "unbundling" in which IBM agreed to price its software separately from the equipment, presumably opening up competition in the software market. While this provision helped create an applications software business independent of IBM, the main consequence was to *improve* IBM's revenue for all its systems software (e.g. the operating system). Another provision was that IBM had to divest itself of the Service Bureau Corporation, its consulting (mainly programming) arm. This kept IBM out of the consulting business for more than twenty years, but had the immediate effect of concentrating Big Blue's attention on its core business which was already becoming too unwieldy to manage.

As late as the early 1980s when I first began to sense that all was not as it seemed, IBM was still a company where growth by every measure – sales, profits, assets, number of employees – was as predictable as the rising of the sun.

Among other things I am a dilettante historian and aware that all empires, no matter how powerful, eventually decay. And it occurred to me that IBM's carefully nurtured image of unfailing professionalism and infinite resources did not imply impregnability. Looked at another way, professionalism and hundreds of thousands of employees can be seen as disadvantages, the former frequently being accompanied by a lack of imagination and the latter degenerating into bureaucracy and waste. Business conditions change and even great companies have been known to stagnate, look at General Motors or General Electric, for cases. Or determine why the A. H. Robins at which I had worked for thirteen years had risen high and fallen low in a single lifetime. While IBM had experienced an impressively long run of success, there was an end of empire flavor about it right then.

The company's senior management, then in its second generation after the Watsons who built the company, seemed bent on changing nothing.

This should not be surprising. As a general rule, the kind of person that rises to the top of a bureaucracy lacks the flexibility and inventiveness of those who built the business from scratch. Their principal goal is to protect what they've got and not screw up anything along the way. If it seems to work, don't fix it, etc. etc. This is a defensive strategy if there ever was one. And "protecting the lead" is one of the better ways to lose the game.

It should be no surprise that the new leaders were more timid than the Watsons.

There are several reasons why successor managements are reluctant to make even necessary changes. First, because such management will invariably be homegrown and such a bird must rise predicated on loyalty to the bureaucracy that fostered him, a loyalty that makes it very difficult for him to trim fat when it is required.

Second, because such an executive is a successful product of the existing order, which means that his personality fits that culture precisely. For him to change that culture suggests that he himself is wanting.

And third, because a mature company is often an institutionalized one and IBM was the institutionalized company *par excellence*. Since the essence of a company lies not in bricks and mortar or voluminous procedures manuals, but in the psychology of the system's advocates, the main attribute of institutionalization is a value system buttressed by a mythology of old business stories. The more entrenched the institutionalized values become, the richer the mythology. In this way it is no different from The Culture and such myths as the character of George Washington, say. In a mature company such as IBM such stories would have been passed down over several generations. It would be used to justify all the successful strategies and none of the failures. And there would be nobody employed there to remember how it actually went down and expose these stories for the naïve myths they are.

For an insider to address the flaws in the existing culture would have been like a U.S. Congressman challenging the viability of the Constitution.

oOo

And so, at a time when the computer industry was undergoing a structural change, at a time when the formulas of the past were being tested throughout our national civilization, IBM was giving a marvelous impression of being a walled-in and timorous empire more interested in protecting its own turf than into venturing into new territory (the Personal Computer project being the sole exception – and that didn't end well).

IBM's mainframe business had already begun to stagnate. While its large system competitors had all died off, it was the decline in growth in the mainframe business as much as IBM's competitive ruthlessness that had killed them off.

Nor had IBM been able to dominate any industry segment other than that for business systems – and it had outright lost one market it once owned, namely, the one for large-scale, "supercomputers". First, the Control Data Corporation and then Seymour Cray's eponymous vector-processing machines became dominant factors in what was then a small but extremely profitable market segment.

Whenever a new computer-related market had sprung up, smaller, more nimble competitors had overwhelmed all the phalanxes and cataphracts that lumbering old IBM could muster.

IBM had never, for example been able to gain much traction in engineering and scientific computing. Laboratories and universities converted to minicomputers at one end and supercomputers at the other. The academic world didn't much like IBM anyway. It was too monolithic, too much the innovation-inhibiting oppressive institution, for the increasingly unconventional university professors that made the academic computing buying decisions. Computer Engineering degrees were just beginning to emerge from Electrical Engineering departments in the more prestigious universities. Computer Science programs, though more software oriented, were being salted by new faculty as hardware savvy as the engineers. As a consequence, the faculties and the newly emerging laboratories and engineering design centers were staffed by very young people, almost always in their twenties and thirties. And young people were highly influenced by the 1960s movements that soon died out in the general culture but persisted in academia through the seventies and eighties and, for that matter, up to the present. The better graduates of these programs didn't want to work for IBM where their status would be lower than the mostly technically incompetent salesman. Besides, they had been taught on very different equipment and computer languages.

Further, minicomputers were significantly cheaper than mainframes and you could buy three or four of the former for the price of one of the latter, thus spreading access to computer power to more students and faculty.

The loss of this business probably didn't seem like much to IBM at the time. Academic, engineering, and scientific computing was comparatively small potatoes when compared with business systems. Scientific computer customers were notoriously price-sensitive, standards-resistant and hopelessly fragmented, there being a dozen or more players in this market. Minicomputers were easy to design and manufacture and inexpensive to market and with so much competition the customary IBM profit margins weren't there. During the era of the antitrust litigation, it might have been an advantage for IBM not to be seen as dominating at least one hardware market.

I might add that IBM's System 3 computers and more powerful versions on the same technical base were not minicomputers, much as Big Blue tried to market them as such. The word "minicomputer" refers to architecture not size. IBM's System 3s, etc. were actually small-business computers, a very different animal.

All of this had changed by the early eighties. The antitrust suit had long since been settled and scientific computing had become the second fastest growing industry market after that for Personal Computers. And with the introduction of engineering workstations and servers using Unix (an open-standard operating system developed by Bell Labs for communications and on-line processing), the scientific marketplace was about to grow geometrically. With workstations and advanced networking engineers could now work collaboratively and never actually talk to one another.

By contrast IBM's minicomputer entries seemed half-hearted and flaccid and its early workstation and server systems were really jury-rigged PCs that made almost no dent in a market then dominated by Sun and Apollo.

oOo

Scientific and educational computing weren't the only emerging markets IBM failed to dominate. IBM had also lost the office automation wars, fallen years behind in networking, and even though Big Blue had set the standard for personal computers, it was beginning to lose market share in small systems, too.

The latter failure had to have been especially galling to IBM since, owing to the marketing push of the Little Tramp ads, the whole world knew IBM was a player in the PC business. And the whole world could see Big Blue lose out on its own standard.

Worse yet, this failure discredited IBM among a group of people it could ill afford to alienate. Corporate CEOS, middle managers, the rank and file now had computers of their own and often these didn't bear the IBM logo. These people had the power to change everything.

At first I couldn't believe that IBM had been humiliated this way. That a start-up company such as Compaq could battle toe-to-toe with IBM and win! What about reliability? What about training? How about IBM's huge network of sales and support people? How could anyone else pretend to compete with a company of a half a million employees?

I hate to admit it now, but as late as 1983 I believed that people who bought non-IBM PCs were naïve fools. Why there were actually people out there who didn't seem to care about anything except that their computer did whatever they wanted it to do at the lowest price possible. Didn't they understand IBM's powerful marketing clout? Didn't they realize they were hitching their wagon to a loser?

If this was what the small computer business had come to, I thought, then the PC was just another piece of consumer electronics like a TV set, for heaven's sake! It boggled the imagination.

And yet…and yet, if you thought about it with an objective mind, there was a certain logic to it all. If a PC were as complicated to use as a mainframe, there was no way all those people would have bought one. If, on the other hand, if a PC were no more complex to use than a VCR, then all a competitor would have to offer was a reasonable facsimile of the IBM product. If a customer downloaded the software and the machine worked the way she was expecting it to do, then she'd be happy. And if it cost less, too, why not buy it?

It occurred to me that locked away in the greenhouse of my IBM data center mentality, I was the naïve one. Perhaps the best pathway into computers *is* the simplest, uncomplicated by all the layers of technology which gave folks like me value. It is Occam's Razor extended to business management.

And if PCs could be made simpler than why not mainframes, too? What could that mean? Might all the rules I'd learned not be laws at all, but only creatures of the need for stability and predictability for computer jocks such as me. Might the computer industry itself be no more than a human creation, not of inevitability, but of happenstance? And what we technical folks saw as the truth be only conceptions that might have been otherwise? After all, barring a few mistakes mightn't it have been Univac not IBM dominating the market?

It is amazing how often I have heard a technician refer to a piece of software as to what it "is" not what it "does", as if it were an uncreated object that emerged from some impossibly competent Olympus.

How, with all my vaunted understanding did I miss this until the mid-1980s when the truth was readily apparent years before?

oOo

I suppose I could console myself with the fact that I had a lot of company in my myopia. Most of my peers were far less receptive to a change in perception as I. IBM's lag in Personal Computers doesn't mean anything, they were telling me, IBM sells the only kind of real computing. Its inability to control the PC business is only a mirage. Why there were a couple of theories being bandied about that postulated that IBM hadn't so much failed as miscalculated.

The first of these, subscribed to by most computer professionals, theorized that IBM's declining PC business was only an aberration, a temporary setback. IBM would eventually find a way to win the PC wars. To those loyalists, IBM's later introduction of OS/2 as the PC operating system of choice was the long-awaited response. Only OS/2 failed, predictably, because the standard, MS-DOS, had already been established. Too late, too late.

The other view, held by a few of the more discerning analysts who knew that IBM couldn't dominate every computer-related market, hadn't in the past, wouldn't in the future, surmised that IBM's PC fiasco had nothing to do with business computing in general. PCs were not, after all, mainframes, couldn't handle multiple simultaneous transactions the way mainframes did, permitted no high-transaction volume data entry, etc. Why the loss of the retail PC business might actually be an advantage to IBM. It might force Big Blue to stick to business computing.

Plausible hypotheses both – and yet neither of them made me feel any less stupid. Fool me once, shame on you. Fool me twice... especially when it is out of an emotional attachment to an idea... suffice it to say that it would be a long time before I trusted my reason in that way again.

Moreover, these answers seemed too glib, too pat, too self-protective and complacent. Something bigger was happening than either theory allowed for. I could just smell it. And that something had implications that went far beyond the PC business. And since I was then employed as a Big Eight consultant, it seemed as if I might turn that insight to my advantage.

And so I engaged in another one of my interminable analyses. When I came up for air several weeks later, I thought I had an answer as to what was the real reason for IBM's PC failure and what it portended.

oOo

IBM had, I concluded, been unable to dominate the PC market by not setting a proprietary standard for the software (forget hardware, software is the most difficult element in a computer system to clone and the operating system which controls all other software is the most difficult to duplicate). Thus, Microsoft was a real institutionalized business from the get-go, while Intel, for all its attempts to market itself as an industrial monolith, was only an engineering firm whose lease on success ran no longer than the most current "hot hardware." As late as the end of the 1980s, it was possible to build a semi-conductor fabrication facility for a couple of million dollars, well within the reach of a Venture Capitalist-supported group of entrepreneurs. Intel had lots of competition. It looked for a while as if the Japanese would control the silicon chip business. Of course, with the transistor density required for the superfast modern PCs, the cost to build a microchip fab facility became infinitely higher. With its huge pocketbook Intel now has a better grasp on the microcircuitry industry than ever before.

Furthermore, it was not by incompetence that IBM was unable to set the PC standard. The IBM managers responsible for the Personal Computer weren't stupid. Their corporate memories extended back to the 1960s when mainframe OS was first introduced and they recalled what that had done to sew up the business computer market. They realized they were taking a calculated risk by farming out the PC operating system to Microsoft. And yet they took it nevertheless.

Why?

Because IBM's management knew that time was not their friend. For this was not the 1960s when the notion of an operating system was revolutionary and IBM had a lock on the business systems marketplace. Back then, IBM's giant product development bureaucracy could be allowed to grind away with no fear of competition beating them to the punch.

But this was the 1980s not the 1960s and there was already a PC industry in place and it was dominated by the Apple II computer with its user-friendly operating system and dozens of software companies clamoring to climb aboard the Apple platform. If Apple were allowed to grow this market for another year or two, there was a real possibility that IBM would no longer be able to compete.

Before Apple, small computers were the bailiwick of hobbyists using such machines as the Altair or the Radio Shack TRS-80. The operating system of choice in that era was CP/M, and IBM proposed buying it. The developer of that piece of software believed that small computers should never be proprietary, a view that was common in the neo-hippie world of computer innovation in that era. This was a view shared by many engineers who perceived themselves in an academic world of papers and prototypes that no one owned. Steve Wozniak, Steve Job's partner in Apple, also thought along these lines. The goal was to contribute some incremental knowledge available to everyone.

How different things would have been without an IBM PC. The business use of PCs would have lagged behind the consumer market. Without IBM's credibility, the PC industry would have grown at a much slower rate. Without the IBM platform Intel and Microsoft would not have become industry giants. The Apple II would have become the gold standard in small computing. It featured a Motorola, not Intel, chip set and its own operating system.

Save for IBM Intel would have become a manufacturer of specialized chip sets at the high end of the computer industry. Andy Grove of Intel had been one of the early developers of the integrated circuit etched on a silicon chip set and had a strongly scientific bent. Microsoft would have remained a small, struggling software firm, if it survived at all. No Compaq, no Gateway, no Dell, no billionaire Bill Gates. And maybe no internet fiasco around the turn of the millennium. A PC industry would have happened anyway but it would have gone a very different direction.

There is a lesson to be learned in Microsoft and Intel's success: Industry giants are not always grown through technical genius or prescience, but being in the right place at the right time and seizing the moment. After all, Thomas Edison lost General Electric and Nikolai Tesla was unable to take advantage of his insights. It was IBM not Herman Hollerith that made card-handling equipment popular.

IBM had plenty of precedent for the belief that a small competitor might become a powerhouse in a niche market such as PCs were then. The dominant standard in the minicomputer industry, which then owned scientific, educational, and engineering computing, was Digital Equipment Corporation's VAX/VMS line of computers. As I've said before, Digital had plenty of competition for their machines. None of IBM's offerings had ever been a competitive factor, though.

oOo

The PC market was not one IBM was going to allow to slip away, although IBM was not all that interested in consumer electronics. IBM, with all its presence at the highest level of corporate management, could see what a grown-up garage shop operation like Apple could not: that small systems had enormous potential in the business systems market.

First, by expanding IBM's presence in corporate boardrooms. The industry was then dominated by the hobbyists, small businesses and spreadsheet addicts, Almost all small system users were techies playing with their machine. Save for Apple, most early PCs were hard to use, principally because they required a very abstract language to do anything. Commonly called "slash commands", so much as starting up the computer was extremely user unfriendly.

IBM wanted to expand into the offices of tens of thousands of senior corporate executives, middle managers and supervisors then untouched by computerization, even fearful of it. IBM believed that, properly trained, business managers might – and eventually would– be sold a PC. If senior management bought an IBM system for its own use, it might strengthen Big Blue's already powerful hold on the imaginations of corporate executives at all levels and maintain its discipline over IBM data centers. If, on the other hand, these executives opted for a non-IBM system, they might be inclined to sponsor a non-IBM solution for other business applications, too, including ones IBM had already laid claim to.

Second, by building new demand for its mainframe business, PCs could replace the millions of dumb terminals then attached or networked to IBM systems. This would permit a new kind of traffic to and from the mainframe. IBM might even win back the office automation business it had seemingly lost to minicomputers. Personal Computers could replace the rather limited stand-alone word processing systems then on the market and still have capacity left over for spreadsheets, presentation preparation and other business applications. Furthermore, PCs could be linked to mainframes to perform such tasks as electronic mail, calendar management, file transfer and data base inquiry.

The new world of computer-based possibilities would be an awkward fit for IBM's existing technology, but by using the Fabian delaying tactics so successful in blocking earlier technologies, IBM might have time to make it all work for them. The business market was then brand new, untouched by Apple and Radio Shack. If past history was any indication, management of internal data centers would wait for years until IBM had product.

Many data center managers were, however, confused by IBM's announced PC strategy. Why a PC when IBM had been discouraging distributed processing for twenty years? (Distributed processing is a way to organize computing where most of it is done locally and only then forwarded to a central data center).

Applications software was no problem. With its enormous experience in business systems, IBM could and did develop its own suite of business applications – and fairly quickly, too. Nor would it have any trouble marketing it. The "Little Tramp" ads were among the most memorable in the history of Madison Avenue.

oOo

Then why the urgency to build a system?

Because to win the PC wars, IBM had to first best Apple at its own game, winning over their base of *consumer* customers. If IBM had learned nothing about the computer industry in the thirty years it had dominated it, it was that the race to set proprietary standards goes to the company that wins the most applications software firms. As third-party products become more sophisticated, the expense of conversion to an IBM platform PC's would become greater with each passing day. With tens of thousands of Apple IIs already in the marketplace and Steve Jobs already conceiving the next generation of system, IBM might lose the opportunity to become the standard in the PC industry if they delayed building a system even a couple of years.

In IBM's internal organization, there simply wasn't time to design and market a Personal Computer. One of the disadvantages of great size is that layers of bureaucracy have the power to slow anything to the speed of frozen syrup. Bill Gates once remarked that IBM's technical development staff was out to build, "the world's heaviest airplane", suggesting that the IBM organization was incapable of visualizing the real, practical goal of a PC business.

Furthermore, IBM was stymied by its marketing first focus. Technicians were demanding to be recognized for their increasing importance to the business.

All those technicians trained on minicomputers were loyal to the technology they had been taught. Thus, IBM had little claim on the best technical talent. When I worked for Digital a few years later, I was astounded by the depth of the technical talent in many different disciplines, such as Artificial Intelligence, process automation, advanced graphics, analog to digital conversion and many others. Not only were they brilliant but a proud bunch also. At Digital technicians were compensated and enjoyed a status little different from the *salaried* salesmen.

Fortunately for IBM, there were a number of microchip manufacturers available. Andy Grove, one of the pioneers of integrated circuit technology, had built Intel into a significant player in chip fabrication. He was very willing to partner with IBM.

Next Big Blue had to buy an operating system. Although the developer of CP/M was too much a 1960s throwback to be willing to partner with IBM, Bill Gates's Microsoft was more than willing to deal. With remarkable *chutzpah*, Microsoft entered the fray without actually having a PC operating system. Gates *bought* the core of MS-DOS from a third party and then adapted it to the Intel chip. To IBM this seemed the best available alternative even though Microsoft retained "slash commands" for many program initiation processes.

The IBM PC strategy of farming out their whole PC with the exception of one small part worked marvelously. Its product came off the mark very quickly and almost as quickly became the *de facto* industry standard. Apple entered into a technical backwater from which it didn't completely emerge until Steve Jobs returned from exile and turned Apple into an applications business in which the Mac fed off the iPhone, iPad, etc. rather than the other way around.

Meanwhile, IBM paid a steep price for its industry leadership in the PC business. The lack of proprietary components opened the door for cloning. Although there was a small internal microchip which IBM owned, competitors were able to copy its functionality with little difficulty. Through a process called "reverse engineering" in which you begin with the developed machine and then figure out how and why it works the way it does, other companies could determine the functions performed by the one proprietary piece of IBM's PC and build an equivalent. This made cloning easy. Even Intel discovered that other chip manufacturers could duplicate its functionality under a closely related technical guise. All you had to do to build a clone was run Microsoft software.

This reduced the PC to near commodity status. In a commodity market it is usually the low-cost vendor that wins. And IBM's huge overhead meant it was never going to be the lowest cost vendor.

Nor were they always the best vendor. Product development teams at small start-ups were not constrained by the complex design procedures dictated by IBM's mainframe-oriented bureaucracy. This meant that Compaq or Gateway or Dell could deliver a superior, cheaper product much sooner than Big Blue. By the time IBM introduced the OS/2 operating system to replace MS-DOS, the dance was over and the cleaning crew was sweeping up the confetti. Eventually, IBM was forced to sell its Personal Computer business that it had done so much to make practical.

Much of this happened after my revelations of IBM's vulnerability in the mid-eighties and even after my "breakdown" that began this book, but I could see whispers of this sea change with the growing power of minicomputers as soon as I became a Big Eight consultant in 1982.

oOo

IBM's PC failure was big and showy and all the more embarrassing because it was visible, but in itself didn't prove that IBM itself was faltering. You can't be an expert in everything, nor can a company compete in every market. This is why conglomerates are usually inefficient. Even IBM couldn't be expected to win them all, although this failure did a lot to shake the confidence of its locked-in advocates.

It wasn't the missed opportunities alone that made me believe IBM was vulnerable. Just as telling was Big Blue's defensive posture against emerging competition in their traditional business market. Since the late seventies IBM had acquired a distressing reputation for promising "vaporware". "Vaporware" is the practice of announcing hardware or software capabilities in advance of their translation into anything usable. Often these announcements were stimulated by competitive advances of other companies that IBM could not match with its own proprietary product. Ethernet, for example, a baseband local area networking protocol, was available many years before IBM's broadband product. IBM was also very late in responding to client-server technology, a product that workstation vendors could deliver as early as the mid-1980s.

"Vaporware" was not the only marketing ploy IBM used to stave off more technically proficient competition. IBM was a past master at technical spin control in which awkward features of its products could be made to seem like advantages.

About this time, IBM increased the intensity of its traditional methods of market intimidation. It used its huge sales and services organizations to crush competition by sheer mass of numbers. And when executives of long-term customers seemed about to hie their way to non-IBM technologies, IBM marshaled a company's internal data center personnel to bully and cajole the still mostly computer-illiterate managers into conformity. Interestingly, IBM remained a significant force in the business PC market long after it lost the consumer market. While one-at-a time sales were not profitable, two hundred-at-a-time might be. Here again, IBM's emphasis on marketing served it well.

The computer industry was becoming too diversified for anyone to control by marketing alone. Every day, it seemed, someone was developing some new computer-related products from video games to advanced calculators to smart data entry terminals (mostly using PC software). From automobiles to vacuum cleaners everything mechanical seemed to be heading toward having a computer component inside. Although it was limited to Personal Computers, which many executives even today believe is a different kettle of fish from mainframes, the average business executive was becoming broadly computer literate. With the cost of PCs and minicomputers being only a nit in a corporate budget, corporate managers were now able to slip these machines through the back door without the usual approval – or sometimes even knowledge – of the internal computer departments.

To the thoughtful observer IBM was beginning to seem like the Dutch boy with more holes in the dyke than fingers.

I wasn't the only one who sensed this. By the mid-eighties the impression that IBM wasn't what it once was had begun to penetrate into IBM's *sanctus sanctorum,* the internal computer departments. For while many data center managers were sufficiently committed to the idea of IBM to continue to await its response to any technological advance, many others were not. Thus, while Big Blue's market share in mainframe business computing remained strong, IBM was not faring nearly so well in the computer industry as a whole.

CHAPTER TEN

I SEARCH FOR THE DEEPER IMPLICATIONS OF IBM'S PROBLEMS

I had a hell of a time convincing anybody that IBM was as deeply in trouble as I concluded it was. When I pitched my ideas to my consulting peers, I met with nothing but skepticism. Consultants are for the most part unusually objective thinkers with every incentive to be receptive to new and unconventional ideas. Little wonder that the CEOS and senior managers in the computer industry looked at me as if I had gone completely around the bend.

In a way I could understand their position. My observations were, for the most part, a reaction to a bunch of trivial business failures, mostly in insignificant markets. At the time IBM's PC business was still going strong.

I once started up a conversation with an IBM sales representative on a long flight. He told me it was IBM's intent to use the PC business as the springboard for even greater dominance in the future. While there were a number of signs of IBM's difficulties, he said, there was no reason to believe any of them were irreversible. Growing pains, he said.

This gave me pause. If IBM's management had recognized the source of its troubles, the company might still be turned around. I would have wasted my energy on a blip on a long upward spiral.

I knew that most computer industry CEOS believed IBM would be able to surmount any obstacle. If I were to convince managers and staff otherwise, I would have to have evidence of a deeper problem, one so endemic that it could not be fixed with all of IBM's resources. One so embedded in the logic of events that even the most committed IBM bigot would eventually see the light.

The only way I could imagine that there was such a problem was as a result of a fundamental change in the rules that defined the computer industry. Managers, for the most part, do not regard symptoms as being indicative of a larger problem. The best they can do is understand fragments. At the time I felt something bigger was there, but all I could see was the grains of sand on a very large beach.

There was, of course, evidence of just such a tidal shift. IBM's defensive strategies added up to a lack of confidence and when a company as rich and intelligently managed as IBM loses confidence, there must be some barrier to its continued success with which it is unable to cope.

It took quite a lot of close analysis, but I finally figured out the big picture that connected all the disparate fragments of evidence. All of the symptoms of IBM's decline, its inability to compete technically, the loss of the PC market, the decline in industry discipline – pointed to a single reality: the computer industry itself was fragmenting beyond the ability of IBM or any other single entity's control. And that fragmentation was a direct consequence of the development of the microprocessor.

In the 1950s and 1960s a mainframe computer was as complex as a weapons system, requiring huge capital resources to design and build. To mass produce one you had to be a giant smokestack enterprise like GE or RCA. At the time all real computers were based on mainframe architecture.

But money, engineering talent and a huge industrial infrastructure were not enough by themselves to allow a company to compete in this industry. As I have implied earlier, the modern digital computer was much more than an engineering marvel used for mathematical computations, but potentially a particularly flexible piece of office machinery. Only IBM had both the capital resources and the business experience to fully recognize this potential.

And recognize it IBM did. By the end of the 1950s, as I stated earlier, IBM had made business systems the standard for computing and itself the standard for business computing. And one after another its giant competitors fell by the wayside.

Nor, except for the Control Data Corporation with its super mainframes and later Cray with its vector-processor based supercomputer, was any new company able to make much of a dent on IBM's turf. So long as the general-purpose mainframe was the dominant architecture, IBM was destined to be the dominant force in the industry.

oOo

Not so with microprocessor systems, where the economy and, yes, the sociology of production was very different from that of traditional mainframes. Of course, mainframes are now also built with silicon chips and IBM is still a very big player in the computer industry, although it has been years since its revenue grew from one quarter to the next. Still, my objective here is to contrast the dynamics of the pre-1980s computer industry that IBM dominated with the new one where IBM doesn't.

oOo

Here, I'd like to pause a minute and talk technical on a subject that even the press struggles with. As recently as a couple of years ago, I read an article that referred to mainframes as room-sized machines to contrast them with Personal Computers and server systems, which weren't. This remark relied on the misconception that bigger implied more powerful. In truth, the opposite is true. A computer's power is determined primarily by the time it takes an electron to go from Point A to Point B. The less time it takes the faster and more powerful the computer. Thus, a huge mainframe can be *less* powerful than a tiny microprocessor system. I remember looking into the large processor/memory box of an IBM mainframe in the mid-1980s only to see… nothing. Nothing, that is, save for a Eurocard board or two stuffed with microchips, which occupied maybe 5% of the box.

In the late 1950s, Andy Grove and others discovered that you could make a much more powerful computer if instead of stand-alone transistors, you could etch them into a piece of silicon, which could quickly conduct electronic signals from one transistor to another (thus, semiconductors). This permitted transistors to be made extremely small. Which in turn meant that the signal between transistors would be received extremely quickly.

I once saw Commander (later Rear Admiral) Grace Hopper demonstrate what this meant by rolling a huge spindle of wire into a meeting room. "This," she said, "is a millisecond (a thousandth of a second)." Then she held up a spindle only a little larger than a spool of thread and much less densely wound. "And this," she went on, "is a microsecond (a millionth of a second)." Finally, she held up a single piece of wire only a fraction of an inch long. "And this is a nanosecond (a billionth of a second)".

The beauty of a silicon chip was that if you packed it densely enough nanosecond speeds are possible and you have a very fast and powerful computer, You could do this through a process known as "photolithography" in which an engineer could design a microchip so that he could read it (I once saw such a design which covered the entire wall of a large conference room) and then reduce the design in size again and again until machine tools could etch the entire design onto a piece of silicon the size of the nail on your pinky.

As is often the case in technology, the early microprocessors allowed for only a few transistors, meaning it was impractical for large scale processing. But the technology developed rapidly.

An integrated chip was also relatively inexpensive. In comparison to the cost of a traditional mainframe assembly plant, the cost of an early silicon chip fabrication plant was quite small. The first such facilities in the sixties and seventies cost only a couple of hundred thousand dollars. As late as the early eighties you could build a modern, fully equipped semi-conductor fab facility for a few million dollars, a sum well in reach for many entrepreneurs.

Later, in the late eighties when the cost of machine tools to etch many, many transistors grew prohibitively high, there were still enough Intel competitors for the industry to remain a technical free-for-all. Interestingly, the computer engineering firms such as Westinghouse and GE, and especially Motorola found they could compete in *this* business.

In spite of the growing capital cost of a fab facility, the unit cost of microprocessors remained quite low, because these miniaturized systems were now practical for all kinds of computer-related applications, from cars to game consoles to vacuum cleaners and other household appliances. Now the cost of a semiconductor plant could be amortized over millions of parts, not just the few thousand it took to sustain the mainframe business.

It might be noted that the processor is not the only chip in a modern computer system. Memory, internal and external communications, graphics, analog to digital conversion, high-level mathematical models (for, say, the weather), all use chip technology. Because the costs other than production and design of microchips remained quite low (raw materials, operating costs, sales), the price of even a very powerful microprocessor remained in the tens or hundreds of dollars.

The economics this dictated had a profound effect on the entire computer industry. Since the secret to profitability lay in large-scale production and the industry leader in performance would have a leg up in demand, semiconductor fabricators had every incentive to translate their improved designs into production as quickly as possible. This led to a technology race in which the latest breakthrough which began at the top quickly filtered to the least expensive desktop model. Since all computer systems were now based on silicon parts, the processor found in the largest mainframe was little more powerful than in a garden-variety Personal Computer. It may be asserted that the PC itself would have been impossible without the silicon microchip.

In response, IBM formed a consortium with Digital and others to achieve a technical breakthrough that would set them years ahead of the Compaqs and Dells. It didn't work.

Chip fabrication and Personal Computer assembly also required a different kind of business organization and worker intellectual skills then the building of a traditional hardwired assembly. Unlike the complex of wires and switches for the most part hand assembled, the microprocessor was a single integrated unit, sometimes including memory, data communications busses and the like all on a single chip. Thus, chip manufacturing was highly automatable, requiring a comparatively small, skilled work force. And it produced a discrete end product which could be sold singly or in large volumes (Mostly the latter, although in the early days there were plenty of tiny shops building onesy-twosy machines. My very first PC was built by a garage shop operation – and worked just fine).

The real complexity of semiconductor fabrication lay not in manufacturing but in chip design (which you have probably guessed from my anecdote about a visit to a fab facility) and the machine tools required to produce the chips. This was a technology that approached the cutting edge of science where only the dedicated mind dared to tread, a mind that could care less about the relatively mundane chore of building an integrated computer system. It's my understanding that the newest computers operate at the atomic level.

All these factors encouraged the development of a semi-conductor industry that was separate from end systems assembly. To my knowledge only Sun Microsystems attempted to do both. This was now an industry in which a vertically integrated, end-user focused company such as IBM could not compete efficiently.

This was not owing to the technology alone. IBM's engineering department was very able to design very high performance systems. IBM's Watson computer was for a while the most powerful supercomputer in the world. And it has become a leader in Artificial Intelligence. Other than these niche markets, however, IBM's tail was twisted by the dynamic change in the *rules* of the industry as a consequence of integrated circuitry.

The businesses that bought semi-conductor chip sets were interested only in reliability, performance and capacity, not in service and support. They could do that themselves, much cheaper than IBM could. For a brief time in the early 1980s semiconductor fabrication was a "hot hardware" commodity business with a number of competitors both here and abroad. It was an industry that was subject to wide fluctuations in demand where profitability was often at the whim of global factors impossible to control.

IBM's shareholders, used to consistent, stable growth, were not about to tolerate the impact on earnings per share that an aggressive entry into this kind of industry would have entailed. To counter these trends and still participate in the computer industry IBM would become a minor player in chip design and production – and would eventually drop out entirely.

The failure to dominate the semiconductor industry meant that Big Blue could no longer regulate the development of the computer industry. Mainframe power would henceforth grow not at a rate gauged to maximize IBM profits, but at a rate commensurate with technological advances in the larger industry. The new types of computer products such as engineering workstations and baseband networking would achieve acceptance not because they were made by Big Blue but because they were the most functional available. Instead of a new generation of computer ever five or six years, as was true in IBM's early days, potential processor power doubled every eighteen months or so. Which meant that IBM's status as a "national treasure" in technology, on which its image as an impervious monolith had been grounded, was no longer a given.

IBM was in a little better position when it came to the assembly of finished machines. Here IBM could depend on its proprietary software and marketing clout to assure its continued control over its well-indoctrinated customer base.

But all was not well for IBM in end-user computing, either. The new silicon chip-based computer system was composed not of hand-assembled wires, relays and transistors but of dozens of chips "stuffed" into printed circuit boards. PCs were internally connected boards into which chips could be "stuffed". Boards were then integrated into a chassis through a fairly trivial production process. This rule held for all but the most powerful supercomputers (very dense computer designs tended to run hot, thus requiring expensive cooling systems). This accelerated the development of a computer architecture that directly challenged the monolithic mainframe's position as the dominant standard, the so-called minicomputer.

The idea behind minicomputers was not new to the eighties; in fact it was as old as the component stereo system. As early as the late 1950s, Ken Olsen, the founder of the Digital Equipment Corporation, had conceived the notion that by designing a computer system in specialized components, he could build one without all the technical overhead of IBM products. Then the one-of-a-kind assembly required for mainframe computers could be replaced by a simpler, assembly line process. And since each component was fully discrete, some could be farmed out to subcontractors to build, which were often very small companies themselves.

Furthermore, by concentrating on customers who prefer to install and maintain their own systems, a minicomputer vendor could avoid much of the cost and bureaucratic staffing of a large support organization. Legend has it that early Digital computers showed up on loading docks with the operating system taped to the chassis. From there you were on your own.

While this restricted the initial market to sophisticated technical and scientific customers, this was a potentially large market, hungry for a cheaper and more flexible option than the ones they had and one that was very receptive to the do-it-yourself philosophy that Digital's strategy entailed. In some cases, users would throw away the chassis so that they could fit a computer into a limited space or integrate it into, say, a series of machines managing a process (process control), such as in a chemical plant.

Minicomputer architecture offered a number of advantages to its customers, not the least of which of which was the low cost per unit of performance, which was a direct consequence of the "scalability" (i.e. ease of growth in capacity or power) of their computers. This was a direct result of the bare bones simplicity of most minicomputers and the simplified approach to business of the minicomputer companies.

The reason for this can be illustrated by the following analogy: Imagine that you could buy an automobile as a bunch of components rather than a finished product. This would eliminate automotive assembly plants and a whole level of bureaucracy and cost. If any part, say the air conditioner, went bad or was obsoleted by a better product, you could replace that product by just dropping the new model into the slot where the old one fit, saving you the cost of a repair. Of course, this is not precisely feasible with automobile assembly, but computers are built more like stereo systems than cars. With component stereos you can drop in a new turntable or replace the sub-woofer merely by replacing the new unit with the old.

When a minicomputer needed to be upgraded, only that piece that required expansion needed to be replaced. (or sometimes added on to, such as memory). In a business where computers were typically obsoleted every four or five years and often replaced due to major upgrades in between, this was an enormous cost saving. (An anecdote that demonstrates the cost of mainframe upgrades: During the early eighties I was offered the space-age front panel of an IBM 370 for $500 cash. And this was the only piece of the machine that was worth anything). By contrast some Digital PDPs are still doing their jobs today.

Scalability also meant that a computer need only be as large as required by the original application. A minicomputer might, in fact, be very small indeed, especially if you got rid of the parts you didn't need and squeezed the individual components into whatever space you had available. One could be hooked up to an existing analog computer or other piece of equipment that was near or at the source of data collection (such as chemical flow) and do its job forever so long as the devices it was hooked to were not themselves obsoleted. Such a computer might never need to be replaced. "If it ain't broke, don't fix it." Unlike a mainframe with many applications, it would never become obsolete. As late as 1985, there were many twenty-year-old Digital PDP computers still in service.

The low cost and flexibility of these machines made them very popular in universities–for education using the simplified BASIC computer language–and in scientific laboratories. In fact, Digital became the system vendor of choice in universities, far outstripping IBM in this market segment.

Still, with the exception of a few companies offering turnkey systems for small businesses or localized processing for larger companies, minicomputers were regarded as way too underpowered for the transaction processing systems typical of financial and accounting applications – and thus not competitive in business computing.

This perception was only seriously challenged when silicon microprocessors became very powerful and the performance of a large minicomputer approached that of a mainframe. Cumulatively, several attached minicomputers could exceed the performance of a large mainframe at a much lower cost. If you could redesign your applications into segments rather than as a centralized whole, you could have a much simpler application. You could also departmentalize applications so that they ran in offices where the source data originated or the finished product was received. Then you could turn the power over the applications to end users rather than some data center in never-never land. This made for a more computer literate staff, which was to everyone's advantage.

This kind of computing was facilitated by the advent of networking in which information could be directly shared between departments with no need for a central computer to serve as a hub. Imagine all computers hooked together with data constantly being circulated by dropping it off at one location to be automatically picked up at another, not dissimilar from the way the bloodstream works. At the time the networking protocol for so-called Local Area Networks (LANs) was called Ethernet or, more properly TCP/IP. LANs could also be connected with WANS (Wide Area Networks) to make a truly company-wide interconnection.

Because computers could be located in many departments, e-mail was now possible. Nearly instantaneous accessibility to data on other computers located a hundred feet or a thousand miles away was now possible All you needed was a dumb terminal attached to your local computer on the network and you were ready to go anywhere.

This conceptual architecture is called "distributed processing" and is in direct conflict with mainframe design with its "all roads lead to Rome" architecture.

A further advantage for minicomputers was that most of their early computers were used for a single application. Thus, customers could replace their older systems with a relatively trivial conversion. This allowed Digital in the early eighties to completely reinvent their technology to take advantage of the new potential for advanced applications with the much more capable VAX/VMS systems.

Sadly for Digital's Ken Olsen and the other minicomputer vendors, the technology ratchet turned once more and minicomputer architecture itself became obsolete. Dumb terminals became smart terminals when PCs could be networked. Soon PCs could deliver the power of a minicomputer on a desktop. Server systems, which are no more than glorified PCs could serve as the data collection hub for information required outside the PC (this is called client-server technology). Client-server technology had been around a while using supercomputers or mainframes as the server. This eliminated the need for the middle man represented by the minicomputer. As a consequence, all the great minicomputer companies have gone away or been transformed. Hewlett-Packard was never just a minicomputer company and has managed the transformation to a being a player in the PC market. Client-server technology has also replaced mainframes in many, especially new, applications.

The minicomputer revolution in systems architectures opened up several new avenues for entrepreneurial activity. First, the building of the end system itself, since Digital was never able to dominate the minicomputer market the way IBM's mainframes had controlled business computing. Prime, Data General, and Hewlett-Packard became big competitors. There were also several much smaller entrants in what was increasingly a fragmented sub-industry.

Second was the development of a computer component market. Because minicomputers were made up of several discrete parts, a company could easily make a better component to replace the Digital original. Disk drives, internal busses, communications interfaces, etc., were often built by businesses that, because they concentrated in one technology, were often more innovative than the general-purpose manufacturers. Digital didn't own Ethernet, thus another company, say, Cisco, could provide better networking solutions. Analog to Digital converters spawned other industries (A to D is a bit too complicated to explain here, but it became a major force in scientific computing).

Third was the building of highly specialized systems to compete with general purpose computers. A small company like Sun could, for example, become an industry giant by building engineering workstations with better graphics and communications. On the other end were restructured PCs which could be made into a server system by linking a number of them together. This was the aegis of client-server technology. And, of course, much more capable Personal Computers.

Fourth were the growth of so-called "systems integrators" (not to be confused with business systems integrators, a wholly different kettle of fish). Systems integrators built specialized systems where the digital computer was only a part of the larger whole. This kind of systems integration began with the space program and the very primitive components of, say, the lunar module. The systems integration concept was the beginning of the incorporation of computers into all sorts of devices, even such common commercial products as vacuum cleaners and thermostats.

Much of this industry change had already begun to occur by the time I started to sell my ideas. The number of bright technical people had expanded exponentially with the much larger number of graduates in computer science and computer engineering now emerging from the great technical universities. These in turn inspired non-degreed technicians who had a knack for understanding the possibilities of computer applications and the business acumen to build those ideas into a company. There were too many technologies waiting to be developed and too many different ways to compete with IBM. There was no way for IBM to dominate the industry the way it had even five years before.

The computer industry *had* changed in a fundamental way. And IBM's business structure – and its mainframe architecture – had not– and maybe could not adapt to these new realities. And yet nobody seemed to know it or understand what it meant. Except for me and only through a glass darkly.

CHAPTER ELEVEN

THE NEW SOCIAL PARADIGM PENETRATES THE COMPUTER INDUSTRY

The popular image of the data center in the early days of computing was as a place of absolute order. This impression, implied by an earlier description, was reinforced by the "display" computer rooms which lay behind a large sheet of bullet-proof glass with curtains that were dramatically opened when guests were brought by the data center. Inside, they would see a room which except for the generally light blue and gunmetal gray machines was absolutely spotless and stark white. The walls, the ceiling, even the flooring which was raised high enough to hide all the cables and wires and other messy components. The printer and the card-reader punch could get a little messy, too, but the speed with which they operated was jaw-dropping. Six hundred lines per minute allowed continuous computer forms to be spewed out at the rate of a dozen sheets a minute. And the card reader-printer could be set to spit out cards so fast that you could not see the punches. Even faster were the card sorters that only read cards and weren't slowed down by card punching, a far slower operation.

The archetypal computer technician was, therefore a man of self-discipline and internal self-control. He was portrayed in films and television as a bespectacled, flat-topped Midwesterner of vague European origin wearing a full-length lab coat and ripping

The Answer off a console printer (which was nothing more than a specially mounted IBM Selectric typewriter). In the background magnetic tapes whirled in high-speed rewind and sorters dropped cards by the bushel into sort pockets. It was no accident that this stereotype was similar to that of the archetypal Engineer of the space program, since both were seen as products of the Information Age.

That the image of the computer technician as a super-scientist was a naïve one was apparent to anyone who worked in a data center for a while. Since programmers constituted the largest number of computer jobs, most people who wanted to advance had to spend at least some time working as a programmer, and programmers never conformed to the Engineering archetype. Further, unlike the stereotype, the real technical people were not usually allowed in the data center. It was staffed by computer operators who were most often mid-level clerical types and were frequently drawn from ex-card handling operators and dressed the part, owing to the messiness of the processes behind the scenes. Thus, the majority of people running around the computer room were low status, having little education beyond high school. And run they did since the various pieces of equipment were spaced wide apart and required constant attention.

In the days before universities offered computer science and business information degree, most programmers were hired out of one of the three pools I alluded to earlier: (1) ex-tabulator operators, (2) internal employees, often displaced clerks themselves, or (3) recent college graduates who majored in anything (although math and business administration majors were preferred). Demand was enormous and starting pay was initially mediocre, although quickly expanding

Not everyone with a degree had the attention to detail or logical inclination to write a program, however, and there were many washouts. But a programming career was a very good way for a smart high school graduate or possessing a mediocre liberal arts degree (like me) to make a decent living.

Few of the early programmers were aristocratic enough in personal appearance or communications skills to conform to the IBM image. Thus, there was very little movement by internal computer people to jobs in IBM–or the reverse.

Programmers were, however, adaptable to the authority and conventional thinking that IBM technology represented. For the most part they were also painfully unimaginative. The few that had a little creativity wound up being systems analysts and determined the functions that a program must perform. Even these were not all that creative and went along with however the previous tabulator system was structured. This limited computerization worked all right in the first couple of iterations of a computer application since an eight-kilobyte 1401 couldn't do that much, anyway. As to the programmers slavish following of direction: this was the early to mid-1960s, after all, and the sea change in the overlying culture had not yet taken place.

The computer programmers who came later, after programming had become a more lucrative career, did have computer-related degrees, but were likewise unlike the Engineering archetype. Computer science majors were usually "numbers geeks", focused on careers at the leading edge of technology, while the Business Information graduates were produced by the bushel-load out of the less prestigious community and state colleges. This did not confer the status of an Accountant or a Marketing graduate, let alone anybody who possessed a BS in Electrical or, eventually, Computer Engineering from MIT or Stanford or Cal Tech. Both degree programs required many hours of exacting labor on homework assignments in messy and overly lit computer labs.

Nevertheless, Computer Science and Business Information systems were very popular degree programs, because there were more technical jobs still than qualified people to fill them and people could advance solely based on their tangible accomplishments. Which was a good thing because few of them fit the image of the back-slapping country club types that formed the middle management of most companies. Furthermore, the law of supply and demand meant that a programmer could often move across town for a twenty percent raise if they became dissatisfied with their current employer.

The downside of such a career was that you could not be promoted outside the data center, because it was believed that a computer career disqualified a person from any other job, so different was their experience.

oOo

The craft of programming rewarded a certain *personality type* that was not found elsewhere in a large corporation.

It was this personality type that prefigured the "tech nerd" stereotype of which we all are familiar. We will henceforth refer to this as the Programmer archetype although there were still many old style programmers through the 1980s. As we shall see, it was not just programmers who conformed to it, but they were the most visible manifestation of it.

That so many programmers conformed to this personality type was a result of the peculiar psychology it took to perform this unique job. For computer programming was *not* a glamorous way to get a quick answer through the incredible speed of the computer, but a tedious and time-consuming means to manage the repetitive processing of data into information.

A single computer program might require thousands of lines of "code", each of which must work with all the others in the program or the job might "cancel" in the middle of a run. And when the program did seem to work, even when it ran all the way to End of Job, undetected "bugs" in the program might mean the results were wrong. To ferret out these bugs a programmer often had to engage in weeks and months of meticulous testing *after* the weeks and months of concentration required to write the damn thing.

And testing was never completely foolproof. Months and years after the program was put into production random errors could crop up, errors that sometimes required emergency repair under extraordinary time pressure.

Programming was such a rigorous skill that many highly intelligent people who tried to become programmers failed or were reduced to writing "quick and dirty" reports. Furthermore, as systems began to drill down into the core of the business during the 1970s and programs became larger, more complex and technically demanding, many older programmers who had once been regarded as competent became marginalized or obsolete (e.g. Autocoder programmers who wouldn't learn COBOL or batch programmers who couldn't convert to on-line). And what was extraordinary about these failures was they didn't really happen because of a lack of talent or premature senescence. They occurred owing to the inability to psychologically handle learning something new, starting over from scratch, and the attention to detail it would take to retrain their minds. Sometimes, a person could not manage having to think for themselves.

To continue to succeed as a high-end programmer it helped to be the sort of person who was turned on by the process of working through the vast puzzle that was a computer program.

Fortunately, not all competent programmers had to advance into new layers of technology, however. Some became systems analysts, a few moved into management, some were flexible enough to move on to new careers. (Although that usually required further education, since very few people advanced directly out of data processing.).

A person who became a good programmer tended to believe in the absolutely objective. No room for mysticism here. Many programmers came to see all of life as a computer program, which if it isn't working for you, must be debugged until it does, including marriages. They regarded those whose problem-solving skills were less systematic than theirs as intellectual primitives, incapable of functioning in their version of the modern world.

Programmers were more than organizers of the chaos of life, they were also creators of an object whose internal design must not only work, it must be "elegant". Often the most admired programmer was the one who could think of a slick new way to accomplish some end whether or not there was any practical value to it.

These types of programmers were always present to some degree. They began to emerge in large numbers in the late 1960s as programmers became better educated and less amenable to authority. I remember one incident in the late 1960s when one of my colleagues attempted to write a simple report program using matrix algebra. It took three times as long to write and nobody else could follow it, but he did it.

Later on, this quest for elegance led to the curious aberration, noted during the Internet fiasco of the late 1990s, of companies that were founded and garnered millions of dollars of venture capital money that a little thought would have proved their idea had no business potential at all. This is also the reason that many high-tech companies have been founded, flamed brightly for a while, and burnt out quickly. The founders of these companies never really wanted to create a *business*, building a *product* was enough. This, of course, was much later, but it was all part of the programmer personality I have described.

Not an artist, precisely this type of programmer was too driven by externals for that (the rules of computer programming did not reward introspection of any sort), he was more of an artiste.

As an artiste he was driven by the desire to create an end product that only he had devised. As an artiste he was intolerant of any bureaucracy that got in the way of doing the job the way he saw it. As an artiste the act of creation so completely engaged him that he had no time to be concerned with personal appearance. Nor was ease of use was much of a concern.

This, of course is the quasi-bohemian ideal that flourished in the late Romanticism that sprang up in the late 1960s. It arose out of the rejection of "bourgeois" values that often signified traditional authority systems which the "flower children" and political radicals were out to overthrow. Although the computer industry was too concrete to have anything to do with the bohemianism associated with *avant garde* art.

As I have already implied, this was also an era of the growing complexity of computer applications as a result of the rapidly expanding power and capacity of the machines. The sophistication of the programming job followed.

The new paradigm also had a number of implications on the business of computing. No longer were programs written to last a year or two. The bet-your business applications such as wholesale distribution or discrete product production control or bank general ledger now had to last ten, fifteen, twenty years. Why some of these "legacy systems' were still operational when the much-overstated Y2K threat presented itself.

Another implication of the new paradigm was the disappearing female programmer. You must have noticed I have used male pronouns throughout this chapter. This is owing to the fact that most of the new breed of computer artistes were men. Early on programming was considered a very good career path for women. It provided much better pay than the traditional women's jobs and much better opportunity for advancement. And if you were any good, you could write a program in a matter of weeks. Yes, there were times where you had to work deep into the night, but this was because of the lack of availability of the machine during the testing phase. And most of these late-nighters were as a part of a team so that some social interaction was permitted.

At one time a good one-third of programmers in my data center were women. And this was not uncommon. Today women are few and far between in the Programmer ranks, especially as you get farther away from the standard business applications of yesteryear. This is because women have far more opportunities in professional and management jobs once the almost exclusive purview of men. Also women are much more social creatures than men and are not ordinarily attracted to jobs where most of their work day is spent alone, often requiring concentrated focus over many months, a focus that makes any kind of social life, much less family life, next to impossible.

Such a concentration requires so little in the way of social interaction and communications skills that some of the better programmers could easily be placed somewhere on the autism spectrum. Over my career I ran into a number of extreme examples of this type. Some could not understand why anybody wouldn't want to figure out complex technical problems. This accounts for the "user hostility" that sometimes creep into PC applications, most especially those programs that are associated with business transactions. Have you ever run into a PC application where you just couldn't figure out how to make it work? Why they don't even supply users' manuals for PCs anymore.

The attempt on the part of early computer entrepreneurs to make users into technicians goes very deep. It's probably apocryphal, but I have heard from more than one source that Bill Gates was unimpressed with the icon-driven user interface (you know what I'm talking about, the little pictures on the screen on which you click your mouse to take you to an application). Even after Apple introduced the first computer using icon-driven technology, Gates resisted following suit. Weren't the slash commands that navigated the applications in early PCs good enough? Didn't people want to get closer to the basic technology? Well, most users don't want to have to struggle to get something done. They just want it all to work.

oOo

Nothing could be further from the ultra-efficient and physically shaped-up Space Program Engineer stereotype than this. Yet by the 1980s the Programmer artiste had become the prevailing archetype not just of the computer programmer but of all the denizens of high-tech industry.

How was it possible that two such diverse archetypes could have arisen out of the same skill?

As I have shown the old IBM-type image was always a bit false. Most internal corporate computer types were not like this, except at the very top. It's true, in the era before casual Fridays I always wore a suit or an expensive sports coat to work as did most of my compeers in the programming, systems analyst, or managerial ranks. In this we were not that different from accountants or salesmen or lower-to-middle management elsewhere in the company. We were just perceived as a little weirder.

But the main reason for the change in perceived image was that paradigm shift again. For the Space Engineer archetype was derived from the older authoritarian concept of project management. In that traditional view, a project was an activity engaged in by a large number of people to produce an end product controlled by one person or at most a small, tight group. In the traditional project every intermediate end product was defined in advance; every end product was purposive, and the only goal that mattered was defined by the project manager(s), who were in control of everything. Not that there was no latitude for tinkering if the original specifications didn't work as intended, but something very like the original plan had to be devised. It was the face of project managers and sub-project managers that were seen by the public and, for the most part, they all conformed to the white-lab coat image (as did scientists and engineers in academia and labs in other fields).

The artiste, on the other hand, creates a discrete product that functions independently of all similar objects (sometimes programmers wrote "modules" of a larger program, but this was looked on as grunt work by the programmers who crafted finished products). While there are loose interfaces with other programs, for example, links to the operating system, most of the program internals were up to the individual. And while the object he creates may be defined by others or is in response to the desires of the user or in context of the work of others writing closely related programs, only he shapes his program and gives it life.

In a project composed of the work of artistes, the project manager is only a facilitator, often with no vision of his own, but with plenty of schedules and responsibility assignments and a feel for whether or not an individual is on target and, if not, if it matters. The project manager's goal is to pull together a satisfactory and timely end product while assuaging the egos of his team. His is also the face of the project to the outside world. Even the overall design is agreed upon by a group or an individual or subgroup especially talented in applications design.

One could not imagine a George Washington Roebling, builder of the Brooklyn Bridge, managing a computer project. A better example of an artiste project manager is an architect who gives way to engineeers.

You might ask which came first, the individualism of the modern day computer programmer or the late 1960s paradigm. My answer is both at the same time. Older programmers rarely resisted project discipline and management hierarchy. They wanted to be told what to do. They rarely questioned received wisdom in their personal lives, either. In my early days at A.H.Robins one of our programmers would wait for everybody else to order at a restaurant, and then order the same thing as one of the others, usually the boss. On another occasion, he gobbled down food that was obviously ill-prepared and no one else touched. When asked if he relished the food that much. He replied, No, I had to eat it fast or I would never get it down. He said he didn't want to embarrass himself by complaining.

But when the New Man emerged, many of the tendencies emerging in the programmer job, the artiste model, for example, attracted him to that career. And because the counterculturals were so smart and so successful, the New Man redefined the technical type.

Thus, a complete applications system of great complexity is almost always a collaborative effort consisting of a number of programs written by several people. It may also include purchased software "packages" to perform some or most of its functions. Sometimes, modules are written by third parties over which the internal developers have little control. Since my program produces end products that are interpreted by yours, the slightest incoherence between the expected and actual output invariably leads to disaster. Furthermore, if my program is late and yours is on time, the whole project may be delayed. Thus, at some point overall project discipline must be enforced. This is why project managers persist even as individual developers chafe at the discipline they enforce.

(This was the best reason I could think of for a company to hire a solutions business such as I proposed for large "bet-your-business" projects. The employees of a solutions business are hired to play a specific role on the project team. Their company is motivated to implement a defined solution so that they might create a reference account that will lead them to other prospective customers. Since the solution is usually based on existing "packaged" software, much of the program code already exists. Any original code created in this process is owned by the solutions vendor. Whatever new code must be created is written in context of the end product not as a stand-alone program. In such a business, individual egos and management *diktats* must give way to the common goal.)

There is a high premium on knowing a software product and all its quirks and counterintuitive features by having used it before. An internal department unfamiliar with exactly how a software product works may waste months or years working through this complexity before reaching the point the solutions company already has in hand.

The tension between self-actualization and systems coherence helps explain the strain between organizational discipline and free expression that infected every computer department I ever encountered. It also accounts for the difficulties that many high-tech companies encounter in remaining viable for more than one or two product generations. As the company expands and the founders grow farther away from the original product, new people must learn the original concepts, people who frequently let their democratic perceptions get in the way of their increasingly fragmented assignments.

One reason that IBM survived its first downturn and remained a major force in the industry was that IBM's core discipline demanded implementation of the controlled kind of change that artiste-run companies found impossible. But there were problems with how they tried to do it, most especially with IBM's culture.

oOo

It was programmers who were first identified with the Programmer Archetype, because it was programmers in high-tech businesses that first exemplified it. Engineering companies were the most extreme examples of this, however, although their employees were much less visible outside their departments. Most of the advancements in computer technology in the PC era are software and thus programmer driven. The "ping-pong table" companies with their work at home ethic, their open office arrangements, and their team decision-making were all a result of the new paradigm. Even CEOs were affected by it, some occupying cubicles themselves.

Which brings up an interesting historical question: How did a personality type that didn't exist sixty years ago come to define an entire industry?

Well, most of the companies in the business were founded less than thirty years before the 1980s and their staffs had grown up during the great watershed of the late 1960s and thus knew nothing but the new paradigm. Often the founders themselves arose from this era and are likely to have been hippies themselves. Some founded companies because they could not tolerate the old authority system. Thus, the new paradigm itself spread the Programmer archetype.

The dominance of the programmer-artiste personality was also aided by a peculiar characteristic of the computer industry: Companies in the industry are, virtually without exception, products of the mind rather than of an industrial process and thus are intellectual property. Intellectual property such as a computer program, like a work of art, is notoriously personal.

This is also true to a lesser degree of internal computer shops.

Thus, while the gifted technician can survive without his employer (he will always be in demand), computer businesses often cannot survive without the efforts of its technicians. Thus, new high-tech companies are usually dominated – and often founded – by programmer-artistes, not by the financial and marketing types that ruled the roost in traditional enterprises. What, for example, happened to Apple when they replaced Steve Jobs with conventional corporate bureaucrats? And then what happened when they brought him back?

But how did the values of the Programmer archetype seep into conventional non-computer businesses and beyond the internal computer departments into the internal structures of businesses and institutions, eventually into society at large?

Because the values and perceptions of all institutions tend to reflect that of their most progressive members; thus, the values and perceptions of the computer industry with its overnight millionaires were seen as a model for their more traditional fellows. Furthermore, since internal computer departments sponsored so much of the company's innovation, it was only natural that its perceptions would find their way into the company at large.

Failure to comprehend the magnitude of the technological change, a number of businesses using sophisticated systems were led into disaster. I know of a company who fired the person most central to its computer success which by this time had penetrated deeply into the core of the business, and it cost them $2 million a year and seventeen employees over several years with poorer results.

Since the values and perceptions we find in our working lives are inseparable from the values and perceptions of our personal lives (we are, after all – most of us, anyway – integrated beings), most people found themselves dominated by the new paradigm even when they were brought up under the old. (But, as we shall see, the social acceptance of the new perception of the truth often predated the adoption of it by business. But when institutions and businesses finally adopted it, it became the paradigm everywhere).

All this spelled trouble for IBM.

If IBM were to maintain its dress code and the corporate image that went with it, it could not make exceptions for technical people, especially those serving customers in the field. As the industry became more pervasive, salesman became less able to deal with any level of detail and technical people became the real business advisors.

Worse yet, in a world where value is often defined by accomplishing something tangible, a sale is painfully intangible. To reward so extravagantly someone who is merely a coordinator... Where is the justice in that? Salesmen came to be referred to by technicians as "suits" or "empty suits".

But it was not just salesmen who were so stereotyped. Other people who dressed in expensive suits and ties and bore themselves with an aristocratic demeanor were viewed with suspicion even when they were technically competent. Big Eight consultants were often satirized for their salesy presentation and paper deliverables. Internal technical people came to despise non-computer managers whom they regarded as illogical and thus incompetent. In some technical circles, the connection between an upper-class appearance and incompetence that a professional appearance suggested came to be regarded as a drag on creativity (the Artificial Intelligence experts at Digital refused to wear ties to customer presentations, for example).

It became a disadvantage for me that I was tall, slender, fit, and looked good in a business suit. In some circles I was dismissed as an "empty suit" or a "face person", even though I had impeccable technical credentials. This added to the difficulties in gaining credibility for my ideas.

Since the layers and layers of IBM middle and upper management had to wear the IBM uniform, they, too, were tarred with the brush of incompetence as soon as they walked in the door. (It's human nature to classify others based on what they represent rather than who they are. In the French Revolution, the Jacobins guillotined even the aristocrats who were on their side).

For their part, IBM salesmen were also dismissive of technicians, seeing them as uncommunicative boffins with inadequate interpersonal skills and without the chutzpah to close a deal if they had to. This mutual stereotyping contributed to the bitter rivalry between technical and sales people which seemed endemic to all companies in the computer industry.

oOo

IBM could not have survived until today had it been unwilling to make some compromises to its well-honed culture. As early as the 1960s, IBM had permitted a more relaxed dress code in its Research and Development Department, for example. And when silicon microprocessors became the standard, every computer company had to manufacture them in special "clean room" environments where the employees had to bathe meticulously and wear special clothing. By the mid-1980s the etched transistors were so small and so densely packed that a grain of sand was an obstacle like a Mount Everest. Even microscopic dust could cause major problems.

But the closer the employee came to the customer, the less he was allowed to deviate from Big Blue's standards. And while this excluded some excellent software professionals from IBM's services and sales support organization, IBM was willing to live with that. After all, technical people could always be trained, couldn't they? As late as the mid-eighties IBM was still restrained by the Anti-trust settlement, meaning applications software development was not legally permitted. When profits from mainframes began to seriously decline, service and support became a major part of IBM's business and the Antitrust settlement was allowed to slide. Unfortunately, when it did, IBM used the same people to build the new services business that had inadequately manned the SE projects before. IBM did not understand the complexity of a bet-your-business development project and had many missteps along the way.

IBM's posture as a marketing company had inevitably led to an erosion of its field technical capabilities. By 1985 the company had become an anathema to many technical graduates, more so the best of them. It was not only the relatively low status of technical people that left a bad taste in the mouths of prospective employees; it was IBM's slow-moving bureaucracy and cumbersome development procedures.

Nor did the talented research scientist believe that IBM was anything special technologically. Graduates of the better engineering and computer science programs were taught on minicomputers not mainframes. Their professors also despised IBM as a company, because they represented appearance rather than intellectual capability. Professors tended to be unconventional by nature and hated business in particular. In the computer science and engineering departments they were busy building a better mousetrap.

IBM wasn't the only game in town anymore. There were too many other opportunities now to make your way in the computer world, including, for the really creative technician, the opportunity to make a killing on his own.

The inability to attract and manage talented R and D professionals inevitably led to gaps in IBM's product line which could not be papered over by all the marketing panache in the world. IBM's software products (and it is in software where the profits are potentially the highest) had always been difficult to use and full of bugs. What's more, IBM had failed to establish any really innovative "platform" since mainframe OS in the late 1960s. All later large mainframe operating systems were a departure on OS, at bottom a batch processing system.

IBM's mid-range business computers, introduced in the late 1960s, a System 3 small business computer using RPG – Report Program Generator as its principal language. RPG had been originally designed to simulate plug-board wiring diagrams on card-handling equipment. This was a technology which harkened back to the late 1940s. They used smaller 96-column punched cards and floppy disks as mass storage. They were sold as monolithic units like mainframes and were not dissimilar in basic architecture to small systems built for many years by Burroughs, Univac and others. It was clear that IBM regarded the System 3 as mini-business systems and not as real general purpose machines. They were incompatible with all other IBM and third-party platforms and could not easily communicate with them. They were not scalable. To get more power or more capability you had to upgrade to the next generation of machine or, if you grew really fast, move to a mainframe which involved a complete software conversion

They were nevertheless extremely popular, especially as Big Blue introduced still more powerful machines in that line–System 34, 36, and 38 and AS/400.

CHAPTER TWELVE

THE NEW PARADIGM TAKES HOLD

A huge and cumbersome bureaucracy and an ageing product line were difficult obstacles indeed. But IBM could have fixed the worst of the unfortunate implications of its approach to technology if it had the will to do so. With all its capital resources it could have created a parallel R and D unit if that's what it took to compete.

What IBM could not so easily resolve was a problem in its technology so fundamental that to fix it meant a reversal in the principle premise by which its mainframes were built. For IBM was wedded to a hierarchical systems design where all transactions flowed to a computer way off in never-never land. And where much transaction processing was performed in batches. Sophisticated users, on the other hand, were demanding that all computers of all sizes talk to each other without a mainframe in between. If you wanted to submit a transaction in Poughkeepsie and right away submit another of a very different type in Los Angeles you were able to do it over the same network backbone (this is called networked computing and is a variant of distributed processing).

This was no trendy whim, either. U.S. businesses felt they needed the capabilities networked computing provided because they themselves were engaged in a historical restructuring, one that would, they claimed, make them better able to compete in world markets, and more particularly against the Japanese. This restructuring implied decentralization of authority and since information tends to flow in the same direction as responsibility, implied the decentralization of computing as well.

It might seem that given enough money and talent, IBM should have been able to fix such a problem with ease. This was no Manhattan Project, after all. But there is a curious truth about computer software development: it is much more difficult to modify an existing system for a new feature than to incorporate it into the original design. A ratio of five to one is a good rule of thumb, provided that the existing system is well adapted to receive the modification.

IBM's plethora of platforms were unusually poorly adapted to networked computing and its mainframe operating systems were so complex that a simple enhancement often took months. New versions of an operating system might require many weeks of testing in the customer's environment before it would work with the same programs. Worse yet they had millions of customers who were not about to change all their "legacy" systems and the old technology had to continue to be supported.

Under the best of circumstances IBM was confronted with many years of patching and making do in order to permit the kind of designs that were truly distributed. This is why IBM resorted to using its marketing muscle and delaying tactics, hoping that it might buy time to force fit the new realities into incompatible technology.

This might have been a successful strategy. There were ways, albeit using cumbersome workarounds, that a hierarchical system might be made to simulate a distributed one. It was just bad luck that innovations in microchip technology occurred almost simultaneously, innovations that threatened to make the mainframe technically obsolescent and much less profitable.

oOo

Was it bad luck?. Or might there have been other factors that made all these seemingly disparate events come together just at the right time to make life miserable for Big Blue?

You can probably tell from the thrust of my argument so far that the answer to the last question is a resounding Yes. It is my belief that nothing in this world is entirely unrelated. In particular, that the inner world of human psychology and the outer world of material reality work with and against each other to produce outcomes that can be predicted and cannot be denied. This is as true for the collective psychology of an institution, a business, or a national culture as it is for the individual.

I also believe that in an era of massive movements, political, social, and otherwise, of mass media, and of powerful institutional organizations, it is most often a collective psychology that will determine the course of our lives. Our own individual values and perceptions are incidental.

This does not mean that individual psychology is not free to form its own path. What it does mean is that an independent exercise of free will had better not take the form of resistance to the collective. It is much harder to select a life's path independent of the structures of civilization, even bad ones, than to go along with the majority. Nor does it mean that the truth is rigid and foreordained. We are reasoning beings that can ferret out a different truth from that of the "conventional wisdom". There is a deeper truth that exists within each of us, but to find it one must disregard the ideologies of civilization and the biases of our own histories. To the degree that our individual personality does not match the prevailing wisdom of the larger culture, we must adapt.

But adaptations have a way of rooting our personalities into a set of ideas and actions which are not authentically our own. To the degree that any psychology is, therefore, artificial, it becomes inflexible to change. Thus, a personality may be well-suited for one culture but be ill-suited to another. The self-same personality that succeeds today may well fail tomorrow. This, rather than a thinning bloodline may be the reason why the son of a great leader so often fails to emulate his father's success.

Not all personalities are able to adapt adequately to a particular culture and some sensitive personalities may not be able to adapt to any mainstream culture. There are always a few members of any culture who don't "fit in", in spite of their competence. When there are enough of these individuals in a company, however, *it* must change if it is to survive. And if there are enough new and adapted companies in the larger Culture, an entirely new paradigm is possible.

Another difficulty with the new industrial culture was that not everyone of reasonable or even superior intelligence could do any job. As systems both computer and organizational became more complex and interconnected, Project Managers, for example, came at a premium. I personally experienced one such failure when a man who had never done anything except administrative jobs tried to perform as a Project Manager without even considering the implications the project had on the computer systems. In such an environment a pleasing personality counts for little.

Although it had surfaced for years, the new paradigm did not immediately become dominant. This is owing to the rule that the dominant personality in any culture seeks out and advances its own ilk as long as it can. An old culture, having been both successful and dominant, tends to be the most inflexible to change. Furthermore, collective psychologies have no capacity for self-examination or reasoned alteration of behavior and cannot change on their own accord.

How then does a new paradigm come to be?

Sometimes it takes a radical shake up in the markets an institution serves or the products it creates. In situations like this, the organization may try to change using the same people and the existing organization. Invariably this leads to failure. The other way is to eliminate underperforming units, or fire the people, especially at or near the top, who cannot change, and force the company to remake itself.

Individually, when something in the material world invades our inner selves, frequently through traumatic events which set free qualities in our personality that would otherwise remain repressed, we must review everything we have done. An adaptation may change the path of our life forever. If we don't have adaptable qualities, we lose.

Similarly, a seismic event may unleash repressed forces in a collective personality by displacing the people that were the mainstay of the old paradigm in favor of those that are committed to the new. The result is usually a violent uprooting with survivors feeling the pain for many years and those displaced never finding as good a job again. This is also why political revolutions are often bloody affairs.

Thus, when great events occur at the same time as a transformation of a culture, it is a consequence of those events that empower the advocates of a new paradigm and marginalize or eliminate those who do not. I am not enamored of the emerging national culture which strikes fear into the hearts of millions of conservatives. But I am well aware that I must accommodate myself to the new paradigm, a very uncomfortable reality.

oOo

And in the case of the new paradigm which began to arise in the 1980s…Well, it had already penetrated into the larger society, especially in academia, in some NGOs, in the relationships between social classes, in many families, anywhere the interaction was between individuals and small groups. Or where a collective personality was by its nature adapted to the new paradigm (as in the ACLU or some computer engineering companies). As an outgrowth of the disorder of the late sixties and early seventies and its rejection of conventional mores, it made its permanent mark in places like Route 128 in Boston, Stanford via Silicon Valley, Cal Tech in Pasadena as well as many left-leaning organizations outside the computer industry.

Ward Cleaver, he dead.

It had not, however, yet penetrated into established businesses, especially the industrial companies in the Fortune 500. It would not be found there so long as there was no seismic event to change the postwar equilibrium. And it would not penetrate into IBM with its unusually rigid and all-pervasive culture. Its dominance of the computer industry and its image of technical imperviousness still maintained its control over the industry and it was not about to abandon that – at least not until there was an event that challenged

IBM's technical leadership in a way that would shake the ideological commitment of its devotees. It would have to happen when the computer industry was ripe for a change.

oOo

What was the seismic event that change the face of the U.S. computer industry?

As in all cultural shifts, it began with a change in the *perception* of the truth. (Perception is reality when you are referring to subjective beliefs). In the late 1970s and 1980s America had experienced economic stagnation. This had occurred, at least in part, out of our declining competitiveness in the emerging global economy. If these trends continued, America would be relegated to the status of a second-rate economic power. This was intolerable. We must emulate those economies that seemed to be successful; we must become more like the Japanese. We must increase the productivity of the American worker.

oOo

Decentralization, empowerment, elimination of layers of management were words in the air in 1985, words all derived from a single idea: putting the people who did the work in a position to make decisions on processes that affected their jobs. This was viewed as the Japanese style of business and the Japanese were seen as the paragons of business efficiency.

Now that Japan is down economically, you might well challenge this premise. But that would be the wrong lesson to learn. Japan's economic troubles result from inferior macroeconomic theory – banking, investment strategy, and the nature of the consumer economy. Also, their ageing and shrinking population, exacerbated by the fact that Japan doesn't tolerate immigration, contributed mightily to its relative decline. The macroeconomic organization into Japan, Inc. was an advantage in an era when Japan had a homogeneous population with a common belief system. It is not so effective when there are insufficient working people paying taxes to support their elders.

Their multinational businesses are still tigers of efficiency, however.

When Japan first emerged as a world-class competitor, it was commonly believed that their formula for success was adaptable only to Japan. Theirs was a highly regimented culture with a well-developed work ethic and sense of national purpose, very unlike the bumptious individualism characteristic of American workers and managers.

Then several large Japanese companies established North American subsidiaries. While they had to make a few adaptations to accommodate the American worker, they never compromised their management principles. This proved that the Japanese style of management could work here as well. It was an example that many U.S. corporations were quick to follow: Quality circles, just in time inventory control, and destructive sampling as the backbone of Quality Control. If any product failed the rigorous QC tests, the whole lot was returned.

Some Japanese techniques worked better than others and more effectively in some companies than others, but the result was almost always better operations and more profits.

There was, however, one important difference between the U.S. implementation of the new business practices from its Japanese model, namely, that the emphasis here seemed based less on procedures and more on management style.

This was not because U.S. business management was unsympathetic to systems. If anything, American management depended too much on systems and not enough on direct observation. It was because many U.S. corporations were already migrating to a more participative style of management at all levels. This trend in turn was owing to dissatisfaction with the old conception of authority, a dissatisfaction that was first expressed by students at the more prestigious universities and then by intellectuals theorizing as to why U.S. industry seemed to be in relative decline.

These business theorists were convinced that slower growing productivity was a direct result of poor motivation on the part of American workers. Often cited were tales of automobile assembly line workers sabotaging their products by slipping a monkey wrench in the front door panel, assuring an eternal rattle. This worker anomie, it was believed, arose out of a conflict between the worker's desire for personal growth and repetitive and mind-numbing assembly line work. This had translated itself into workers' feelings of insignificance and dissociation from company goals and a consequent breakdown in job performance whose symptoms were manifold: absenteeism, drunkenness and drug abuse while on the job, active flouting of authority. But most of all, resistance, to any job content which might increase productivity and reduce the need for workers. This resistance translated into rigid and sometimes absurd work rules set by negotiations with labor unions.

It is very possible, even likely, that worker anomie was not the only reason for poor productivity. The national collapse in inner cities caused by white flight, led to a much different work force in many established factories. Closing down plants in unionized inner-city neighborhoods and moving them to small ununionized towns in the South or overseas did wonders for the production costs of, say, General Motors. Resistance to labor unions in these states and in most offshore locations and a much more pliable work force willing to work for a significantly lower wage meant that products could be built much cheaper than in the Rust Belt. The Japanese companies building plants in the U.S, started out in southern small towns, such as Nissan plants in Smyrna and Shelbyville, Tennessee. This suggests that some of the reason for the relative decline in productivity lay in the nature of the work force, independent of the national culture.

It didn't matter; even in business perception is all; the notion that the old sort of authority was obsolete and that a new more participative authority system was needed was much more comforting than the view that the entire society was in the process of social collapse. It was more comforting because the mass culture made it so.

Management theorists believed that worker motivation might be restored if the openness and democracy that had already occurred in the larger society was translated to the work place. Now that college students were beginning to evaluate their teachers and even participate on the Board of Visitors; now that mass culture was recognized as high culture; now that elections and even legislation were being influenced by public opinion polls and focus groups; maybe workers could be trusted to assist in defining the conditions of their work.

Democratic worker involvement was exactly what business theorists with the assistance of consultants and internal managers began to implement.

The new paradigm had already begun to work in high-tech businesses, especially the newer minicomputer companies. This was mainly because many of the employees were highly specialized and their loss would be temporarily disastrous. It was also because of the engineering mentality which despised any attempt to set up some employees as better in kind than others.

Digital Equipment Corporation featured cubicles rather than offices for all employees except for managers of people. The few private offices were quite small, allowing only for two or three person meetings. Area Managers had a little larger office, allowing for a small conference table and a larger desk and storage area. Larger meetings were held in one of the many conference rooms.

All employees were salaried; salesmen were not commissioned. Workers were classified into one of three groups: salesmen, technical people, and managers. Each classification had a system of ranks and each level in one group had an equivalent in the other two. A junior level salesman was roughly equal to a software services systems engineer and a branch manager in sales was classified along with a branch manager in software services and a major account manager with a systems consultant. At each level the pay salesmen and managers received was only slightly more than the software services employee. A branch sales manager would be paid a little more than the software services branch manager. Also, the software services manager did not report to the sales manager. Unlike at IBM, there was no such thing as a unitary branch manager. It was very possible for a software consultant to be paid more than his branch manager. All this made for a very egalitarian and flat organization.

One oddity of the Digital system was the relationship of pay to billing rates. Since branch software employees had to help defray the cost of every level above them, their billing rate was significantly higher than an equally paid employee at the Area level. This made no sense since the Area level employee was, for the most part, more experienced and more competent than his compeers at the Branch level.

oOo

Thus, the most important consequence of the adoption of the "Japanese" business structure was not in the practices themselves, but the increased involvement of the rank-and-file worker in the business process. In Japanese companies this was largely limited to assembly line workers. For administrative workers, the effect of these procedures was almost the opposite of that in a true industrial democracy. There, managers were a kind of feudal nobility, separate from and superior to the rank-and-file. The goal was to rise in business management so that you didn't have to work as hard. European businesses, on the other hand remained radically departmentalized, accounting rarely talking to manufacturing, for example. There the objective was to protect one's barony from losing responsibility to someone else's.

In the U.S. there was quite a different consequence to these changes, much subtler, which took much longer to work through, namely, a fundamental change in the roles of supervisors and managers.

oOo

Almost from the beginning of organizational reengineering, it became obvious that the decentralization of decision-making rendered many levels of management superfluous, if not counterproductive. These layers had grown up for many reasons, but generally reflected the view that leadership goes to the person with the better technical skills.

The best athlete gets to be the Quarterback; the best accountant gets to be Controller. Thus, managers were expected to *do* rather than merely shuffle paper and accept progress reports.

Now that the rank-and-file employee was a part of a team of more or less equals, there was little need for a supervisor in the traditional sense. A manager may be supervising people whose actual job skills he or she might little understand or be able to perform. Most project managers became mere facilitators. Leadership, to the degree it was required, would emerge from within the work group.

It was equally obvious that this new organizational structure was brimming with opportunities for increased profitability and productivity. Elimination of layers of authority meant the laying off of numerous middle management and supervisory jobs (and associated cost) as well as a decrease in the time it took to communicate between senior management and the person on the firing line. In theory, anyway, companies could run much leaner.

All those middle managers had, however, served a real purpose. The best of them provided a consistency of management practice while allowing for human variety among their subordinates. More time was permitted for training and building interpersonal relationships.

The old style of manager was often a promoted peer of the rank-and-file employees that they supervised and trained. Working outside their job description was encouraged if it led to improved practices. Most training was on the job even for white collar positions. The old style manager helped integrate new employees into the company culture, rewarded the outstanding employees (and not just at performance appraisal time, either) and punished the laggards. They were rarely called a manager unless they supervised two or more subordinates. They were, in a word, manage men(t).

The new style of management was built around job descriptions where the new employee was expected to start on the job with the requisite skills already in place. One need learn only the specific skills required to adapt to that specific company. Often, the office employee was expected to be as circumscribed in his job as the work rules limited a union employee. It was much better for your career if you were *not* creative or innovative but followed standard industry practice or the latest trend in management theory.

The new breed of managers were systems managers. With huge spans of control – a manager might have thirty direct reports – systems managers had little time for regular face-to face interaction with members of their staffs. Instead, they managed through paper – progress reports, expense and task reports (where the employee justified her pay by logging the time spent on previously agreed upon activities). Also, various types of (hopefully objective) management analyses, and that old bugaboo, performance appraisals. The latter grew from a two or three page annual document, rating predefined categories, to a complex process involving the meeting of objective goals with regular reviews. This led to the hiring of a new breed of staff specialists who assisted managers in the design, modification and maintenance of the systems needed to monitor the performance of their departments. It also resulted in a new type of administrative assistant, far more powerful than the secretaries of yore. These new specialists carried out many of the communications, training, and coordinative chores once performed by managers themselves. Management was now a technical skill – repetitive, clerical, reactive, and often divorced from the day-to-day reality of the function managed.

Another implication of the rise of the systems manager was the *spread* of business trends, or new management techniques, complete with buzzwords and authorized texts. From time to time a new business trend swept through American industry like some kind of infectious disease.

Now, those of us who spent their careers in the computer industry are very familiar with this sort of thing. In fact, the business computer originated as a business trend whose adoption was a necessity whether or not cost-savings ensued. Standard programming languages, data base management systems, on-line data entry, report generation systems, all began as practices that *had* to be adopted by the well-run computer department.

The reason for all this focus on methodology rather than results lay less in the quest for efficiency than in the psychology of the technician.

The technical personality wants to believe that there is a magic formula, which if adopted, will invariably lead to success. This goes along with the view that life itself is a computer program, a concept with disastrous results. There was always the hope that in the next whizbang methodology resided the elusive magic bullet.

It should be pointed out that many of these methodologies were no more than a rehash of the way many people had been doing things all along, embellished with the sophistication and glitz that appealed to managers. A classic case of putting old wine in new bottles. Frequently, these processes were so complicated that hardly anybody could manage them let alone implement them. This also applies to general purpose business processes that didn't necessarily involve the computer. None of this should be a surprise since these new techniques were often packaged by academics.

The archetypal computer systems manager was remarkably like the archetypal programmer (no surprise here, most systems analysts had been a programmer early in their career). Like the programmer he believed that there were techniques, in this case management practices, that would eliminate the uncertainties of this disorderly world. And, like the Programmer, he was inclined to disregard human factors in his assessment of the viability of the "new" practices.

This was, I'm afraid, one of the consequences of MBA case studies extended to the practicalities of business management – and of the growing and necessary systemization of business training in general. (Necessary because job training is no longer accomplished informally by a manager, but formally, before hire, by a University or technical school).

It was an unfortunate trend since if one is to understand human relationships in a business setting it is not enough to take a course in systems management: one must also become a *Humanist*.

Business trends also opened up many opportunities for well-paying business careers. Learning the ins and outs of a business trend established one as a business guru, able to command hundreds of dollars an hour in consulting revenues and many thousands more in speaking engagements. Business trends also provided well-paying employment for thousands of management consultants who had become qualified to recommend and implement them. One of the consequences of all new practices, including the soft technology of management theory is to provide job security through specialized knowledge.

Business trends often generated huge revenues for software firms. By the end of the millennium business trends were almost always supported by computer software, another indication of the close connection between the Programmer archetype and the personality of the systems manager.

All this sometimes served to benefit American industry – and sometimes didn't. One thing's for sure, however, it made the large corporation a very complicated enterprise indeed.

This had implications on IBM's structure and competitiveness. The fact that it invented few of these business techniques made it superfluous in assisting and managing these new theories. Most of the software required was developed and run on minicomputers or later PCs. One unfortunate implication of the new style of management was that it tended to regard employees as "human resources" composed of definable skills that were as interchangeable as there were people with the right skills available. The only "real" people were the few that a manager worked with every day. Even those were disposable no matter their talent so long as there was a ready pool of people with the right paper credentials.

The senior management of the enterprise were also systems managers. Thus, it became much easier to inflict a ten percent "across the board" personnel cut than to fire an inefficient secretary. Or to paraphrase Stalin, one person laid off is a tragedy, ten thousand is a statistic. This sort of psychological distancing encouraged "down-sizing" and "restructuring" so prevalent since the late 1980s, where companies were able to temporarily improve profits by laying off large numbers of people (an avoided cost, you see). Temporarily, I might add, because this kind of blind, massive reduction in force was all too often followed by a gradual increase in employment to replace needed skills. But, of course, these were different people. The old loyalists were gone.

CHAPTER THIRTEEN

THE NEW PARADIGM BEGINS TO AFFECT BUSINESS DATA PROCESSING

The one fed off the other: the new leaner management style had profound consequences on business data processing while the new capabilities of small computer systems made decentralization more effective. Thus, what first appeared as a change in management style alone, wound up being a redefinition of the nature of management itself. What began as a mere accommodation of existing systems to the new management structure eventually led to a rethinking of the very nature of business data processing.

Although internal computer departments were able to treat the new style of organization as if it were simply a problem with report distribution, one that could easily be accommodated by installing a couple of remote printers in offices that didn't have them before, it soon became clear that such a cosmetic change wasn't nearly enough to effect a behavioral change of this magnitude.

Only complete functional accountability would allow the new company organization to work. And functional accountability would never be complete so long as the "all roads lead to Rome" batch processing model remained in place. Clearly, businesses would have to make their systems facilitative to the individual's work, as the new paradigm seemed to insist, rather than to a single independent power base, as the hierarchical bureaucratic organization had allowed them to be.

Now there are certain responsibilities which *ought* to belong to a centralized data center. Design of the backbone network is one; establishment of hardware and software standards is another. What is much less clear is the amount of control central departments should exercise over the development of systems or the management of applications that required specialized skills such as Artificial Intelligence or data mining.

In the older, hierarchical world, centralized control was absolute: Users might enter data remotely but the central computer crunched it, managed the computer files and distributed all the reports and documents. As late as the mid-seventies most central computer departments functioned this way.

This led to a paradoxical inconsistency in behavior on the part of computer center personnel: on the one hand they were resistant to the exercise of executive authority, on the other, they were reluctant to relinquish their authority over system users.

Many non-computer executives had already sensed that the power of the relatively lowly computer department personnel radically undercut the existing company hierarchy. As early as the late seventies many computer departments had been forced to allow users a say in department priorities through steering committees. Individual users were allowed to be part of development teams, in some cases becoming the Project Manager. Such practices were, however, usually half-hearted and often ineffective. They did little to restore the control to end users–and did nothing at all to accommodate the more inclusive management style. And it is easy to see why: users were ill-equipped to deal with the jargon and complexity of the development process. Nor were they able to keep up-to-date on current practices even in their own applications.

Frustrated by their inability to control their internal computer departments, whom they regarded as unresponsive and unconcerned with their business needs, corporate executives often vented their spleen on data center managers. As a consequence, many otherwise people-oriented companies went through several computer department regimes in a matter of a few years, only to find themselves worse off than before (owing to the loss of experience in existing programs and systems). Tapping into this frustration also led to untold bonanzas for large consulting organizations, who might understand standard industry practice but spent years figuring out a company's specific needs

If users were to exercise control over their systems, and thus over their day-to-day operations, they would have to do more than participate in applications design, they would have to make the policy decisions which dictated the design. It is policy and organizational decisions that define the direction an application will take when computerized. And it better be right before you lay down the first line of code. Once defined, it is next to impossible to change the fundamental direction of an application or change the assumptions of a single program. When user department people replaced computer center personnel as project managers, they had to learn the sometimes counterintuitive stumbling blocks to every decision they wanted to make. This is why the development process involved several increasingly detailed deliverables and why the process required sign-offs at each of the dozens of checkpoints.

But control over the development process was not enough by itself to return control of systems to the users. For the principle source of the data center's power lay not in the systems design, but in its control over the trove of information locked away in the data center. As long as internal computer departments regulated access to that data, end users could not hope to control their destinies – and without that, they could not hope to control the operations of their increasingly information-driven departments.

oOo

The easiest way for corporate management to reduce the data center's control was to move the computer files off of the of mainframe onto systems in the various user departments. And then give that user the tools to enter, process and access the information in those files (distributed processing).

The central computer department often raised an objection to this kind of decentralization, an objection which seemed on the surface to have some legitimacy: Hadn't there been one overriding reason to centralize data, namely the technical expertise and ability to control standards?

Not really, as it turned out, since control over data quality can best be done in the location from where the data originates or is modified, in short, the place where the clerical massaging of data is performed. Where standards can and should be set centrally, it is best enforced by the dynamics of the system itself, where a non-standard computer or application invariably shuts the user off from corporate-wide systems or those in other departments,

As for technical expertise...well, to the degree it was needed at all, it could just as easily be rented from a consulting firm or a service bureau. Much of the complexity of centralized applications was as a result of their size; keep it localized and ordinary people could master much of the technology, even programming. This decentralization was only fully realized by the Personal Computer.

Then why had data processing ever been centralized?

There were a number of historical reasons for that, the paucity of technical talent in the early days of systems development for one. Also, most applications of any size were mainframe organized even before they were computerized, as I have shown earlier. And with the limited power and capacity of early machines, companies had little incentive to build sophisticated interdepartmental applications that required expensive machines all over the place. Most of all it fit well with the hierarchical business structure of the era.

There was also something called Grosch's Law being bandied about back then. Grosch's Law stated that the cost of a unit of computing was inversely proportional to a computer's size. Or to put it another way, an application ran cheaper on a big machine than a small.

Grosch's Law only applied to the special circumstances in the technology of early computers. More recently, it has been replaced by Moore's Law which states that the number of transistors that can be packed on a microchip will double every eighteen months or so.

The more transistors in a given space, the faster an electron can move between transistors. The faster an electron moves, the faster it can perform a unit of work.

The main reason for centralized processing, however was the hierarchical organization of the era. Take that away (which decentralized authority implied) and offloading the mainframe might not be as risky as you might think.

Once you accepted the notion that offloading the mainframe might be a good idea, then you opened yourself up to a whole raft of speculations as to how computing could expand its reach into new areas of company operations.

oOo

All the organizational and technical difficulties I have just pointed out had a number of positive implications on my proposed consulting business.

First, an organization focused on one group of applications had no dog in the fight between user-based and centralized data centers. It would be motivated solely to design the best application possible for that user. They would allot adequate time to train the end users to operate their own systems, something that internal departments had been loath to do.

By assisting in the decentralization of applications, they could also increase user knowledge of computing itself. This would help users understand the ease or difficulty of a specific change and the need for a lengthy testing process. It might also give them the ability to conceive of ways applications could be improved.

Since consultants are hired and paid for by a company, our consultants would automatically acquire more power than the internal department. What manager wants to admit that he hired and paid for a dud?

Senior management would have to become more involved in functional decision-making in order to be certain that their money was being well spent and that the new application served the company as they envisaged. They would be less likely to fire their internal computer management and/or staff since those persons would have limited control over the project and could not be blamed for a perceived lack of progress.

Suppose, for example, a company has a number of stock-keeping locations. What would happen if you took the inventory system off of the main computer system and installed it on individual computers at each of these locations? Why have reports at all? Why not obtain the status of the local inventory by inquiring on line into the inventory file, which would be as current and up-to-date as the last transaction? Why not make the information on that file instantaneously available through a network to everyone that needs it, no matter how remote they are? How about making a checkpoint image of the file (say, daily) available for processing throughout the network? Wouldn't it be better if shipping and ordering data entry were performed by the shipping and order clerks at their work site? Not through dumb terminals, but directly into Personal Computers that could purify data as it is entered?

All this technical talk brings up another objection to distributed processing: were the functional managers really capable of the technical expertise necessary to run a computer facility, even given the fact that a distributed application was more forgiving than a centralized one? If functional managers were theoretically capable of managing their own their own data center, wouldn't that responsibility add irrelevant chores to an already overburdened manager?

If they were able to wrestle with technical responsibilities, would they remain sufficiently up-to-date on the rapidly changing technology to design tomorrow's applications?

Take the questions I have just posed. Didn't posing them require a great deal of technical sophistication, the kind which traditional managers, charged with day-to-day operating responsibilities, uninterested in the details of technology, and cowed by the jargon-rich data center personnel, had rarely possessed? Would user management, now begin to think computer strategy as well?

With the help of the central technical facility, they could. There were two main strategies that sometimes worked. All design and programming could be performed by the central facility and then implemented piece by piece across the country (or world) by employees of the computer department who understood the implications of the revised procedures. Or the central facility could transmit the changes to each office and allow them to install it. Remote users could also write stand-alone programs for their branch alone.

It turns out that the strategy you used depended on the size of the distributed office. If these branches were fairly large, the company could afford a person or a small cadre of people to maintain the base systems, write unique applications, and operate the computer(s). The development of core systems would remain in the central data center.

Very small branches where a technician could not be afforded would require a central technical person to install new versions of the system. This would necessarily require a phase-in period where installation and training would be accomplished in individual offices over a period of weeks and months. Since some offices would be running the old version and some the new, the flexibility to change the basic structure of systems would be limited. Clerical staff would operate the system which had to be functionally simple.

In this scenario the central data center operated like a plumbing contractor, who would install and repair the pipeline (systems), but nobody needed a plumber to turn on the tap.

As to the routine operation of the system in the branches– and this is how company restructuring began to take on a life of its own – the new breed of corporate managers was used to thinking of business issues systematically. Brought up on statistics and objective analyses, he thrived on the capabilities of electronic mail, desk-top publishing, spread sheets, automated calendars and the like. But most of all he wanted access to the data his department required. These could only be accessed by use of a Personal Computer hooked up to the departmental processor, and most of this required an advanced network that linked computers both within and beyond his own branch. The fact that IBM was late in the networking business was another reason why its platforms lost many battles to control the industry.

The newly computer-literate manager was now able to ask the tough questions as to the design of business applications. He was not only prepared to broach them, but also, for reasons of his training, experience and personal aggrandizement, inclined to visualize them as running on a computer that the central data center did not control. He disliked going to the central data center hat in hand and beg for improvements.

Control of his own data had many consequences on the work life of the systems-type corporate manager. As he began to gain experience with distributed applications, he began to see ways to combine the outputs of these systems with the text and graphics available on his PC. He began to manage *by* information instead of *with* information.

The burden of an extremely wide span of control could be lessened if a manager could communicate with his subordinates and peers at his leisure rather than in a formal meeting or at a time convenient to both himself and a subordinate. Why his subordinate need not even be in the same physical location for him to work with him every day! Without the need for face-to-face communication he could better filter the information he received before he needed to respond to it. If he needed an *ad hoc* report to make a decision or present a case to his own management, he could get it in a timely and professional manner.

There were, of course, several downsides to the new paradigm. The increasing dehumanization of worker-management relationships has already been noted. And the intellectual requirements for the systems manager were much greater than those of his predecessor. No longer was personality the acid test for a supervisory position. "Anybody can do any job, so why don't you hire your friends" was a forgotten phrase. Now you had to be competent in more than day-to-day operations.

I recall a conversation many years ago when one of the middle managers at A. H. Robins responded testily to a junior executive who was an acquaintance of mine. My friend had complained that his new job was mainly clerical. "Clerical", the older manager said, "Aren't most executive jobs mainly clerical"? He was right...back then.

More problematical still was the *type* of intellect that made a good systems manager – task-oriented, problem-solving, never late with any assignment, very good at anticipating the desires of the higher ups. His was exactly the kind of intellect that got good grades in college. His was not, however, the sort of intellect you looked to for a creative solution in a crisis. Nor was he especially effective in understanding human relationships, an absolute requirement for the more strategic forms of reasoning.

The easy availability of technology was not an unmixed blessing for corporate managers or their computer center equivalents. By the late 1980s computers had penetrated so deeply into corporate management that electronic mail could now be sent and received twenty-four hours a day, seven days a week. If a manager had twenty or thirty direct reports and his supervisor had a dozen or so, not to exclude exterior managers and peers, then the number of people with whom he communicated on a routine basis might easily number in the hundreds. This meant the queue of messages he had to respond to, important and trivial, urgent and less so, might easily grow to thirty or forty a day. Weekends, holidays, vacations. He was never truly off the job.

Because he *could* create more sophisticated reports and more professional-looking presentations, he had to. These documents and displays became huge, exacting productions, requiring man-days in the preparation, man days that too often were spent in the off-hours when he had nothing else to do...like raising a family. The systems-type manager was one hell of a hard-working individual.

As you might imagine, this also meant that companies structured like this were radically different in organization and individual job duties than the more relaxed management style of the past. It necessitated an advanced telecommunications network run by protocols like Ethernet in which messages could be routed directly to the recipient through a totally interconnected backbone without their ever going to some centralized system as was a necessity in the mainframe world. With such a system a message could be dumped on the line with a recipient's address and go through the net until it reached the recipient's work station where it would be "picked up".

oOo

In the mid-1980s this was only a conception, implemented in a few companies. By the millennium this was the reality that was implemented in every company and in most individual home workstations. That all this happened so fast was a shock to me even if I knew it would happen someday.

My vision in the 1980s was that computer networks could be used to facilitate the Japanese management style. (This was not the Japanese administrative style, however. When I consulted with Calsonic, a parts subsidiary of Nissan, in 1984-85, the Japanese middle and lower managers were huddled in their cubicles until the wee hours, fingers flying over their abacuses, making up special internal reports similar to the ones the U.S. managers were producing out of their computer systems. The Japanese management style so successful then was a means to control inventory costs, production line management, and quality control not to produce analytical reports.)

Not all of the technology needed to support my vision was then available ...and even less was actually implemented in any workable form. The crude early versions of distributed processing involved freestanding remote computers which transmitted data files to a central system once or twice a day, a far cry from the sophisticated "work group" computing which emerged over the next ten years or so.

Only a very sophisticated organization would have tried to implement the kind of technical environment I perceived was necessary. Not surprisingly, universities were the best audience for such ideas. A few businesses did convert to fully distributed systems despite the fact that the supporting business organization was not yet structured to take full advantage of the new technology. This hybrid organization of computing was part of the vision I promoted then, knowing it would eventually become obsolete, yet moved in the right direction.

○○○

I am forced to shake my head here. Was I so anti-humanist as all that?

I can excuse myself by claiming that this direction was inevitable, not necessarily what I wanted to happen. But this would be a lie. I really, badly wanted my vision to work out. Why? Because I didn't particularly like the exercise of traditional authority. It had given me heartaches throughout my life. Besides, I thought my vision would be implemented by humanists like me, the techies were not imaginative enough to do it right.

It didn't turn out that way. The implementation of new technologies was accomplished by the new breed of "techie" visionaries who could care less about the end users. Most humanists were quickly weeded out. Often, rightly so, because humanists didn't want to understand the technical details as I had. As a consequence, we have the fallible, self-serving, often brutal computer universe we live in now.

○○○

Then there was the matter of IBM's resistance to the new technology… and what that meant to my plans. Which brings us back to IBM's difficulties in adapting to the distributed processing world. Was it, as I stated at the beginning of the last chapter, all that difficult for IBM and all its resources to convert its technology?

Well, as I have earlier pointed out mainframe technology of the early 1980s assumed that data would flow into a central hub and then flow back as processed information, most often in the form of printed reports.

The "all roads lead to Rome" strategy of managing data lay, I knew, behind the design of every mainframe computer. In particular, it was the way IBM's 360 platform had been built. *All* other current IBM products (with certain negligible exceptions), whether software, peripheral equipment, even its small business systems, were designed to work with hierarchically built technology. All announced *future* products–including those that might have supported networking–were presented in context of this platform. IBM's few true minicomputers were, on the other hand, half-heartedly marketed and technically cumbersome.

IBM's way of doing on-line processing used a system called "polling" where the central computer periodically checked each connected workstation in sequence to see if it had data to send. Then it would grab all available data at once. The minicomputer's way of doing the same thing was to have the remote terminal send its data to a specific port on the computer, character by character or packet by packet. The trouble with IBM's way was that all transactions were handled by a single program, called a teleprocessing monitor, underneath which the data management programs for all online systems would run. If one of these data management programs failed, the whole system would "go down". This was called a "storage violation". If there were twenty attached users each with its own application, and one went down, nineteen other users would be interrupted simultaneously.

The non-IBM standard was to let the operating system invoke each on-line program directly as if it were just another batch program. If it failed only that program would fail. All other users would be unaffected.

There were many other disadvantages of IBM's non-standard on-line approach, which are too numerous to recount. But this one was, in my opinion, the biggie.

Further, IBM had no incentive to make networked computing work. PC to PC meant fewer transactions going through the mainframe, meaning slower mainframe sales. If networked computing were to become the dominant technology, mainframes, which continued to represent a huge market would be a shrinking part of an ever-growing pie.

And by 1985, it was clear to me that the decline of mainframe platforms was exactly what was going to happen. This led me to conclude that there was a huge opportunity to build a big, new technology, one source of my plan.

If I was right...and I could see no way that I was not...IBM was faced with a whole series of technical quandaries which boiled down to the most basic dilemma of all: How was Big Blue to convert away from a hugely profitable, but obsolete hardware design without sacrificing market share. Especially given the fact that that there were thousands of users with hundreds or thousands of programs each, all of which would have to be converted.

Unless IBM could defuse the vogue for distributed processing or offer some competing technology of its own, its supremacy in the industry was likely to become at best a primacy. I could see no way IBM could practically maintain its supremacy. A primacy might be feasible only if IBM offered a networked solution of its own. This would involve Big Blue's building a wholly different technology from the obsolete 360 base, and that would require users to rebuild their applications from scratch.

How was IBM to go about a reversal in platform philosophy when that meant a slow and excruciating conversion for all of its users? And a reversal of everything it had been preaching for thirty years?

It could deal with the marketing problem easily enough, since this was merely a matter of psychology and IBM had always been brilliant at manipulating its users' belief systems. Sure it would be embarrassing for Big Blue to admit it had been wrong about distributed processing, but it could call its product by some other name and tell its customers it was different from traditional distributed processing even if the end products were exactly the same thing. IBM loyalists were sure to go along with such a ruse. Its APPC (Advanced Peer-to-Peer Communication) was a solution IBM came up with, very late in the game.

But how was IBM to accomplish a reversal in philosophy with existing technology? Wouldn't IBM be better off cutting its losses and creating a completely new platform that would compete against its own existing mainframe architecture? Other companies had done it, Digital Equipment Corporation for one.

But most of its PDP machines had been used for a single application. Those could be left in place until there was a reason to replace them. As late as the mid-1980s thousands of PDPs were still doing useful work.

Most IBM mainframes, on the other hand, ran multiple applications which had been laboriously built and enhanced over many years. These applications usually involved many programs each, all running within the same box. More than a few companies had structured their business operations around these systems. If IBM were to convert to an entirely new platform, twenty years or more of technical infrastructure would have to be abandoned, not only its own but that of all its customers and suppliers.

Try to imagine what that would have meant. Imagine telling customers that tens of billions of dollars of investment in applications development was all of a sudden obsolete. Imagine the products of dozens of software firms suddenly becoming unmarketable. Then imagine all the internal computer staffs (a big company might have a thousand or more computer-related jobs) having to learn brand new technologies. The thought of such a change was mind-boggling.

No, I concluded, improving the IBM mainframe platform might entail great cost and no little inefficiency…and years of continued delay, but replacing it would be unthinkable, since there were already large minicomputer companies with many years of experience in developing new platforms that were clean, complete, and much easier to operate. That was a risk Big Blue would never take.

The dirty little secret in computing, one that a lot of people knew, but nobody seemed to understand, was that mainframes were no longer all they were cracked up to be economically. Compared to a mid-size VAX, a low-level IBM mainframe delivered a pitiful price performance ratio.

This is even more so today when a $1,000 desktop system can out perform the $5 million processor of a couple of years ago.

CHAPTER FOURTEEN

A SUMMARY OF THE TECHNOLOGY DRIVING THE COMPUTER INDUSTRY

This was an exact reversal of the situation in the early days of the industry. I have earlier referred to the premise known as "Grosch's Law", which, to reiterate, stated that the bigger the computer, the cheaper it is to run your program.

In those days a more powerful machine meant a physically larger machine. The IBM 1401 computer that I operated required the better part of a computer room wall to house its sixteen kilocharacters of memory (yes, I do mean 16k) and half a dozen tape units. A really big computer (say, a 7090) and associated peripherals might require a space the size of a medium-sized haberdashery. During the subsequent 360 era, when technology became more sophisticated and systems used space more efficiently, a 360/65 was still much more massive than the 360/30 and infinitely more powerful, Grosch's law still applied.

The huge physical size of early mainframes was a result of the way computers were then built. Magnetic core memory, stand-alone transistors and cabinets full of wiring required an enormous amount of space. Further, transistors densely packed grew very hot. The largest machines required special cooling units over and above the standard computer room air conditioning units.

Computer systems of the era were built as a monolithic whole where only a small portion of the machine was the processor. The wiring for memory, internal and external communications, etc. was the biggest component of the cost to build one. It was much cheaper to buy a single system with a more powerful processor than multiple smaller systems. Thus, the quest to design more powerful… and physically bigger mainframes. Furthermore, communications between systems was difficult, making it nearly impossible to integrate applications between machines in a seamless flow.

Even today this seems not to be common knowledge. Even today, you will read a business journalist referring to mainframes as room-sized machines, as if this meant great power that, of course smaller systems couldn't possibly match. Makes you wonder who's managing your money, doesn't it?

So when the microprocessor chip was invented and enhanced to the point where transistors could be made very small and densely packed on a thumbnail sized piece of silicon, computers could take a quantum leap in power with greatly reduced cost.

This was not the only implication of semiconductor technology. For virtually all elements of the central computer could be similarly miniaturized; Memory and internal communications could also be fabricated using this same technique. Further, all similar chips could be mass-produced. Even mass storage could be similarly miniaturized.

Despite the extraordinary economies available through semiconductor technology, it had little immediate effect on the price of mainframes or their sales. Early machine tools were severely limited as to the number of transistors that could be etched on a single chip, which meant that it took a large number of chips to build a system. To build a reasonably sized machine, a good deal of individual assembly remained. Furthermore, even the biggest CPUs weren't powerful enough to handle the new more comprehensive applications that were then being developed. Even mainframe systems were being built containing two, four, and sometimes more processors. This is called multiprocessing and required a more sophisticated operating systems than could be written for a PC. The trouble with multiprocessing technology is the operating system overhead was so great that at a certain point the next incremental computer would slow the system down. This was a very small number–eight to ten processors, depending on the applications mix.

Parallel processing was believed to be another solution. Unlike multiprocessing, parallel systems could permit hundreds of interconnected computers with little decline in overall performance. The Deep Blue computer which beat chess champion Gary Kasparov was a parallel system.

Conceptually, a parallel system operates by having a central front-end system that serves as the input controller and feeds data to the first tier of computers. Once the work is done there it is sent on to the next system where another part of the application is executed. The next computer could be next door or dozens of processors away. In that case the data would have to flow through a number of other processors to get there and some of those processors might be doing work that would temporarily block the pathway. Do too much moving data around and the parallel system will slow to a crawl. But build the right application with the right internal design where long-distance data moves are minimized, such a system can function in aggregate with all the power of a supercomputer.

Such a system can be quite cheap per unit of processing power since Personal Computer chips can be used as the individual processors. Each processor would not need a full version of an operating system, but only a "kernel" to manage the expected input, supervise the processing, and determine the direction of the output. This was 360 era stuff, requiring a small fraction of the resources of a mainframe operating system replicated eight or ten times in a multiprocessing system. Thus, a parallel computer lost very little power in having a dozen, a hundred, or a million processors.

But there was a huge limitation to parallel computing; it was deucedly difficult to program. Thus, most parallel applications were the only process that ran on the machine at any one time. Such processes were enormous number-crunching applications, such as weather forecasting, chess or Go playing or non-destructive crash testing. Many of these jobs were variations of Computational Fluid Dynamics (CFD).

I might add that there were many other designs for parallel computers, and what I describe above is only one of them, the hypercube. But all parallel computers operate under the same constraints. Even today, parallel programs are prohibitively complicated to write. First introduced in the 1980s, parallel computing remains a niche market. IBM is a big factor in parallel computing but the implementable applications are few in number. Good for demonstration purposes it has done little to grow the company.

The technical problems with building a PC that was truly competitive with a mainframe continued into the 1980s. Although you could by 1983 or so build a complete personal computer with huge external mass storage through a Winchester technology that was nearly as capable as mainframe disks and sell it for a hundredth of the price, mainframe computing remained the standard. Because of the general perception of microsystems in the 1990s as individual freestanding *Personal* Computers, PCs were regarded as desktop machines for a single user. PCs were unable to displace minicomputers until the very late 1980s. Digital Equipment Corporation had its best year in 1987, for example.

Another factor in computing in the 1980s was that, unlike today where every year-or-so processing power doubles, the speed of computing seemed about to hit the wall at a couple of megaflops (million floating point operations per second, floating point calculations being built on a logarithmic measure peculiar to scientific calculations). To avoid this seeming stumbling block several solutions were proposed. I shall mention the most important four. First, the use of non-silicon materials, which at first offered great promise, but proved to be unstable in practice.

Then, RISC (Reduced Instruction Set Computing) was conceived of as at least a stop-gap measure. Sun Microsystems was the principal proponent of the RISC idea. Much of the instruction set built into computers in those days were used for business processing only. Since Sun built engineering workstations (similar to PCs but used very differently), they felt they could dispose of the business only instructions. Fewer instructions meant a faster computer.

Loading graphics to a specialized CPU could reduce the power required for central system graphics processing, leaving the main computer with much additional power.

The development of client-server technology was another PC processor saver. In the early days of this technology, a mainframe or a supercomputer rather than a specialized server system could serve as the hub. Sun Microsystems was a pioneer here, too. Client-server technology was used initially to allow users to have their own computers and transmit the results to a centralized server system. This was like turning mainframe processing on its head.

All these new technologies were facilitated by faster and faster microchips. Although the cost of a microchip fab facility had grown significantly as the years went by and their complexity grew, the applications for them grew much faster. As a result, a small group of engineers could build a large company strictly on their own brainpower. A person could become wealthy overnight with the next great thing. IBM was unable to compete with this sort of dynamic. There was no incentive to build such a technology in a large company owing to the bureaucratic overhead in big companies versus the small cost in people and machines to build a system in a small one. By the time IBM recognized such a market, it was already too late. IBM was never very good in copying someone else's idea.

The reason IBM was able to retain its market share through the 1980s and into the 1990s lay in all those computer programs in that huge box off in never-never land. The cost (and risk) of converting all that software was prohibitive and highly risky to boot. It was much easier to let your mainframe applications grow than to force distributed processing on a refractory technology. Hence, the illusion of IBM's continued prosperity despite its technical obsolescence.

There was, however, an alternative to the dilemma of mainframe versus Personal Computer (or minicomputer or engineering work station)…and that was to choose both. Instead of automatically developing new applications or replacing legacy systems that had outlived their useful life on the mainframe, you could rethink them as networked applications.

You could let Personal Computers absorb as much of the applications load as they logically could, then forward to the central system only that part of an application required for availability at the main office). Or you could continue to centralize processing for applications that must be coordinated with other users.

You could, for example, automate transaction processing at a teller's window, then transmit the day's work to the central system for the daily bank General Ledger. Or you could enter an order at a remote site, pull the merchandise, prepare the shipping orders and bills of lading, print the invoice and transmit the invoicing and inventory information to the central computer for integration into credit management, sales reporting, national inventory management, etc..

An alternative to moving the applications at one fell swoop was to convert the applications off the mainframe individually at a time convenient to the computer department's schedule. Or at a point when you are about to explode out of your current mainframe (most IBM customers had to upgrade their systems every three to five years). Instead of buying a new system why not buy a dozen or so small computers instead and find ways to offload some parts of existing applications? And save yourself a couple of million bucks in the process? For a few prescient users in the mid-1980s (and quite a few more today), this was a legitimate question.

This is where I'd come to in 1987:

I'd seen what could be done with networked computing and understood what it meant, at least in theory. And it was all bad news for IBM. Frankly, I didn't see how Big Blue could possibly survive long term, let alone retain its historic growth rate.

What's more, I seemed to be the only person around who fully understood the consequences of all these changes. (Admittedly, I was dealing with a very small sampling of experts, namely, my management consulting peers at Peat Marwick). Surely, I thought, I could figure out some way to make use of these insights.

Of course, I was ignoring the lessons implicit in the earlier chapters of this rather long discourse on IBM and the computer industry. I had let the enthusiasm of discovery outweigh the knowledge of IBM's enormous resources and its powerful image. IBM's was power constructed into a company culture so comprehensive that it constituted an ideology. Like all ideologies (and to continue an earlier metaphor, all religious dogma, too), IBM's was constructed on the human need for rootedness in a community of believers. It was an ideology which had a grip on the imagination of an entire industry and much of the country, too.

CHAPTER FIFTEEN

HOW IDEOLOGY IN THE COMPUTER INDUSTRY LED TO REJECTION OF MY IDEAS

I don't hate IBM: I never did. In fact, I rather admire Big Blue. Sure, it emphasized a Machiavellian *realpolitik* in its techniques of manipulating the market rather than technical excellence. But why would anyone expect more? When you get right down to it a company is in business for only one goal: making as much of a profit as it can. It's true other companies in the computer industry were motivated solely by building the slickest products imaginable. But most of them paid the price sooner or later for a lack of concentration on earnings.

It's true the quest is to make a profit above all is a cliché – and a cynical one at that – but the moment we forget the quest for earnings, the moment we glorify any business, the moment we invest our self-worth into an ideology, is the moment we are truly lost. Further, any legal means to maximize earnings is fair game.

IBM's marketing system was a damned sophisticated way to that end. The miracle of it was that its marketing strategy was, for many years, not in conflict with delivering a really fine product, especially during the 1960s and 1970s when computer industry growth depended on a single standard for each system component and supporting software. The public committees established to do that were often years behind the curve. Thus, IBM's proprietary standards served that purpose. The country needed an IBM then.

Thus, if you have assumed that this is another expose of an aggressive behemoth, a Hollywood notion of the big evil corporation, then you are dead wrong. I am no anti-capitalist polemicist.

Nor is this the work of a Wharton School MBA type, no searching objective analysis of business practices, no Peter Drucker-like attempt to define the problem or improve the breed. This is history, pure and simple. If there is anything in this book that attempts to define the future than I'm barking up the wrong tree. If there is anything relevant to the present here, if there is any guide to the future, then it's merely the book's defining principles that might apply to future situations. It is more a description of IBM's inability to cope with a new industry paradigm and what that meant to me.

Thus, this is also a personal history, written through the filter of my consciousness, and if at times emotion leaks through, then that can be enlightening, too. Emotion is often a perfectly rational reaction to the stress between ought and need.

The abstract ought is cerebral and individual, while the psychological need is sensuous and universal. Thus, while abstraction explains, only the concrete engages the understanding. Try reading the empiricist John Locke's *The Essay on Human Understanding*. Locke so distrusted "poetic expression" his work is almost unintelligible to the lay reader…and yet his ideas themselves are not all that abstruse. A little subjective personality, i.e. emotion, inserted into a tract often makes the abstract intelligible.

Sometimes I need a little emotion to force me to take a stand (or more precisely, force me to express an opinion I have already developed psychologically). Because of my timidity, I am often loath to expose myself this way, out of fear of seeming irrational or, worse yet, of appearing to have not thought things through. Then I wind up becoming one of those fence-sitters I talked about earlier, the sort of person who joined a fraternity in college, because the bohemians seemed to wear their unconventionality on their sleeve. A fraternity brother of mine who ended up being a fiction writer, described me as, "wishy-washy".

To the true believers I appeared colorless, without personality, and ideologically wrong. They didn't trust me. I was too cold, too factual, riding two horses at the same time. Yet when I do take a stand, it is with such passion that I seem another person altogether. That befuddles them, too.

That's okay, I don't warm up to ideologues, either. They are too quick with answers, too instinctual with their responses (why must everyone be so consistent?)

It must make it easy to have all the answers at your fingertips, really comforting to be quick with an authority for your position. The confidence these people exude! It often intimidates me until later when I get a chance to mull it over. And they grow so emotional when you confront them with their hobby-horses. The truth has to lie with the way they think it is; so totally are they invested in it.

It occurs to me that there is another consequence to being an ideologue. Again, the stress between ought and need. "Ought" is an imagined reality, a Utopia perhaps. "Need" is the desire for truth to be found in facts. This struggle has to be doubly intense, because underneath the imagined reality is the very different structure of real existence and underneath the desire for the facts to be the whole truth is the human emotion which distorts belief and makes the hobby-horse necessary to begin with. The only way, it seems to me, that one can deal with this tension is either to live entirely in terms of an ideology, which institutionalizes a form of ignorance, or to live forever in a state of perpetual rage at those who refuse to comprehend that there might be other views than their own.

Now those who think of ideology as something like Marxism or Fascism, something European and discredited, must wonder what in the heck I'm talking about here. You may not know anyone you might classify as an ideologue.

I have a much broader conception of an ideology than you might be used to. In my view it is any single idea from which a whole vision of reality is constructed. Given this definition, ideologies are everywhere. (I think they are inevitable in a world that worships systems). Any concept around which a system of thinking is formed qualifies. The notion that the Bible is literally true is an ideology around which many other beliefs are founded. The belief that social ills can be solved by some kind of universal system is another. So too was the notion that IBM was impervious to any threat to its hegemony.

As a matter of fact, the values and perceptions of any collective psychology must eventually form an ideology. If they were not then we would not have the cultural paradigms into which we have fit ourselves over time. It would make no sense if it were otherwise. It would never form a collective psychology, a mass culture.

An ideology must appeal to one's emotional needs as well as one's intellect. The arguments for an ideology are crafted to be logically consistent and intellectually defensible – but they are always pat and brook no challenge, all contravening facts aside. If one is to subscribe to an ideology one must never examine its presuppositions or its appeal to the psychological needs of its adherents. It must be allowed to seep over a person like the spangled quilt of Mother Night.

Each corporate culture constitutes an ideology in a general sense. None was ever so pervasive as IBM's. The industry culture of the IBM-related software and services companies had one, too, namely, the perfection of the IBM system. Further, the perceptions and values of the new paradigm emerging in the larger Culture are also founded on an ideology unheard of fifty years ago, namely, the conviction that there are no gradations of value and that we are in some sense all equal.

Thus, when we are not in fact equal, the losers in the game of life are made to feel deprived and the winners guilty and much of society wishes to redress the balance. This accounts for the periodic emergence of Socialism which can never succeed. Post-Modernism is merely a more sophisticated version of Socialism, but Socialism as it applies to all the many cultures in the world. It too fails as a system because it too discourages innovation. Who would take the risk and waste the time in creating a new order of things if there were not extraordinary rewards for her efforts?

This is not to say that the rewards shouldn't be proportional to the value-added. But the poor will always be with us. We cannot realistically create an absolutely equal society in our nation without impoverishing all. Let alone worldwide. The Soviet Union is a classic example of this.

oOo

It's tempting to get sucked into an ideology. There the answers for all the complexity of civilization are available; there the community of true believers is longing to welcome you...and it is painfully lonely without one. I, for one have more than once been seduced into the jaws of enthusiasm...only to be spat out like a bitter rind because sooner or later I'll come to my senses and ask the wrong question. It's all right to be cynical but skeptical, never.

Socialism is particularly seductive for those who have learned to be computer technicians because all computers that have the same nomenclature on the box are indeed the same. Many conclude, as I have pointed out before that the human brain is just another computer. The advocates of Artificial Intelligence believe that a computer will soon be devised that is more capable than any human brain. Maybe, but my money is still on the biological brain when it comes to creativity.

My skepticism inevitably brought the wrath of my former colleagues on my head. When challenged, ideologues will either try to intimidate you into submission or they will purge you.

The reason that most people remain committed to an ideology whose essence they only imperfectly understand–and few truly understand the source of their convictions – is that the ideological group in which they participate defines their sense of being. Without it they are quite literally nothing. Thus, when you question the beliefs that form the root of an ideology, you not only challenge the idea itself and the conception of the world that it entails, but the self-perception of its believers.

Ideologues will react to your skepticism by attacking you as irrational, by logically and cogently demolishing your notion of reality through formulaic premises which seem all the more true because they are a reflection of tightly circumscribed and internally consistent conceptual universe. And if you are not confident in your views; if you are not an ideologue yourself, you believe that you yourself are in error. It is far more comforting to give in to their opinion or take an equally irrational opposing position than to come down in between.

In my opinion you are most honest with yourself and with some hope of understanding the world as it is when you regard every idea, every conclusion as contingent and subject to change when new information comes to you. And there is some degree of the truth out there for you to plant your stake. These are called facts.

The computer industry of the 1980s was, as I have tried to demonstrate over the last few chapters, particularly susceptible to the ideological kind of thinking. These were systems implementers, for the most part, people who believed in a point of departure and a stable body of knowledge. In this very chaotic and transient world, there was a natural need for eternal verities (even if eternal meant one's working life alone). The IBM way seemed just such a rock of permanence, one that explained all and controlled all, in the computer industry anyway. And, of course, there was IBM's marketing system feeding the idea that it did.

Thus, the idea of IBM the omnicompetent had become one of those keystone views where it seemed you had to be an orthodox believer or a heretic. If you bought into the idea that IBM was selling (for the most part my target audience did) then you were committed to a whole series of beliefs about yourself and the nature of the truth. If you didn't, you had to believe there was something fundamentally wrong....power corrupts and all that.

When I reached the idea that IBM was no longer the company it once was and revealed the consequences of its monopolistic business tactics, I pleased no one. The pro-IBMers were quick to suggest I had a personal vendetta against Big Blue even though I had worked with IBM technology for more than twenty years. On the other hand, the anti-IBM lobby maintained that I had come around to their way of thinking too half-heartedly and too late, probably because I was too conventional-looking, too starchy, too articulate, and not nearly technical enough to grasp the obvious.

I was neither for nor against IBM as an institution; my objective was not to discredit IBM, only make use of what I knew about its out-of-date technology and social organization..and the development of systems.

But in a world dominated by ideology, mine was a very problematical position to take. I know this now as I did not then. In a world of polarities, all alien forces are the enemy.

oOo

Unaware of the pervasiveness of the ideology I was proposing to overthrow, I prepared my presentations as if my audience were the recipients of a consulting report, mainly factual with a bit of enthusiasm and humor thrown in. In addition to a visionary and high-level conceptual picture – I didn't want to flood my audience with uninteresting details – I salted my slides with literary allusions, citations from scholarship and analogies from history. Especially history, since I believed IBM resembled nothing so much as a dangerously over-extended empire.

Once more I had miscalculated. Computer industry people were not interested in vision, they wanted custom and prior practice. They often designed their systems based on how other people had successfully implemented theirs. Worse yet for me, if they thought of the lessons of history at all, they believed them irrelevant to the current situation, the modern era being radically discontinuous from all that happened before. Empires no longer weakened and the law of entropy was no longer applicable. Progress was always linear.

Being the tinkering technical sort, industry executives focused only on making the future a better present. Most hated the arts and were willing to tolerate learning only for its utilitarian value. How to build and how to make, accounting practices, or the law perhaps. Maybe economics in the sense of how the company's activities fit into the larger economy…and little more.

Thus, my pedantry and visionary flights left my audience more than cold; it offended their sensibilities. Rather than communicating the deeply thought out case I believed I was presenting, my hard-won analogies seemed yet another reason to reject my ideas. Especially when it came to my beliefs about IBM.

"Nobody," a young non-IBM marketing analyst once told me, "ought to dismiss IBM's ability to overcome any obstacle." Many I talked with responded with the old industry saw, "Nobody got fired for recommending IBM." They averred that IBM was composed of preternaturally clever people who did and always would maintain an iron grip over the entire computer industry.

Later when IBM had temporarily come back from the abyss – although it had become a very different business–it was this reputation for competence and power, sometimes deserved, frequently not, which preserved its position even when technological logic suggested otherwise. It had taken the hiring of the first outsider CEO in the company's history, Lewis Gerstner, who emphasized software and services rather than big boxes, to turn the giant mechanism around.

The fact that he was able to do this when IBM was ill-prepared to enter these industries demonstrates how persistent IBM's impervious image was.

Back when I was making my pitch, before IBM had gone through its first spate of bad times, and there was no tangible evidence that I was right, who could blame my critics for not believing me when all I had to offer was a vision.

oOo

IBM did not fall by the wayside. The truth is I never expected Big Blue to collapse entirely. I knew a number of business applications where batch-type processing worked just fine. My proposal was instead predicated on the belief that the rules that IBM portrayed as eternal verities were not and this would have a profound influence on the structure of the computer industry. I believed that I could help a computer industry company survive and maybe even prosper in the aftershocks.

My counter-intuitive perception that the IBM way was not what it once had been was not the only reason my proposal was rejected. How could it have been? The main thrust of my ideas had nothing to do with IBM. My observations about Big Blue were only a door opener, a means to instill a sense of confidence that I was on to something, as well as to communicate a sense of urgency that many companies needed to replace legacy systems soon.

And make no mistake about it, a number of IBM-related software and services companies also needed to modernize and expand their offerings even aside from Big Blue's decline, whether through aging product lines or slower revenue growth in the industry as a whole. Quite a few IBM-related vendors were seeing a slackening demand for their products. One or two had already begun to look to ways to alter their business practices. Such as supporting other platforms instead of merely IBM mainframes. Or being willing to take on larger projects in their support organization.

But even the executives who had sense enough to realize that change was inevitable were put off by my proposals. Why? I beat my head against the wall. Why?

I at last concluded that it was that cultural thing again. The left-brained rigidity of a management that had succeeded according to a formula they understood, partly owing to the conviction that the business was what it was because that was the way it was supposed to be. (This was a tautology if I ever heard one). But most of all owing to their unwillingness to contend with the opposition of their employees.

I had already figured out a way around the employee resistance factor, hadn't I? If I had my way, most of the rank-and-file would barely know I was there. How could their managers still dislike me so?

CHAPTER SIXTEEN

THE FEAR OF TECHNOLOGICAL OBSOLESCENCE ALSO WORKS AGAINST ME

This was the question that rattled through my brain that night in 1988 as I pulled my Merkur Scorpio out of the parking lot underneath Colony Square in Atlanta and drove out into the rain-slicked streets. I mulled this question over all the way to my house in the Atlanta suburb of Alpharetta. It obsessed me as I ate my supper without tasting it and stared at the television screen I could not see. I came up with no answer, not for many weeks, and not in all its glory until now.

When my wife asked me if I wanted to go upstairs to bed and instead of answering, I repeated her question. In a moment of embarrassment at the absurdity of my response, I momentarily dropped my concentration. I looked into her perplexed, exasperated face. Only then did I at last understand the core of what I had been mulling over for so many hours. Or rather accept the unpleasant truth I had been suppressing for weeks.

"How could they dislike my message so?"

An image came into my mind of a man jiggling his knee. An executive who had listened to me...and jiggled his knee.

oOo

It then struck me. Managers did not dislike me *per se*. They distrusted the unconventionality of my ideas. Of what my proposals did to change their tight little world. No matter how I tried to disguise it, no matter how I attempted to sugar-coat it, my ideas represented a discontinuity and implicitly a rejection of so many current practices.

And that meant insecurity for them. If what I was saying was true and their business would have to change so radically, how could the same personalities that had been so successful in their existing business adapt quickly enough to find a place in the new order? There was every reason to believe that many of them could not, because my approach implicitly depreciated the value of the technical skills and product knowledge that was all the unique value these people possessed. The rank-and-file were the fertilizer that made the business grow. A software product is never static. It always depends on regular improvements. This requires exceptional people working many years, building their competence, and are thus hard to replace. A services business, on the other hand, depends less on continuity with a product and more on a continuity of business practices.

Technical people were notoriously independent and resistant to outside forces. Just my presence in a company with a license to implement change might have led valuable people to resign just at the time their skills and company history were most needed. Those that stayed, frequently because they were fearful of not being able to change, were likely to become angry or depressed. Productivity would decline. It was much easier to adapt the process to the needs of the staff, rather than the other way around.

These were well-founded concerns, I later found out. It was the resistance of the consulting staff at Integral, a payroll/personnel software company that eventually sealed my fate.

Here is where we came in many chapters ago with all the talk of resistance to changing the company culture and before my long ramble on the vulnerability of IBM. Back then I alluded to a second factor operating against me in selling my ideas, namely, the conviction on the part of computer industry executives that the only kind of people they needed were the ones they already had. These were people who "knew" IBM technologies and the products and/or services sold by their own firms.

When I thought about it that night in 1988 what a discouraging insight this was. I was not only competing against the idea of IBM but against the entire monolithic culture and belief system of the entire computer industry. It could not, would not be changed. (except, of course for the kind of gradual changes dictated by improvements to technology) unless they failed on their own.

While my predicted changes – and more – did eventually occur, they occurred more outside than within the existing industry. And they occurred in a very different way than I so prematurely proposed.

I was not surprised that technical employees, charged with the responsibility to implement change, would instead be the first line of resistance against it. I had dealt with this reality all my working life. Years before, I had given this aberration a name, technological insecurity.

Technological insecurity among the technical elite is less of a paradox than it might seem to be. For there is a mean reality to being a technical person – or having any job in the current climate. A person's economic value is totally dependent on the scarcity of her skills and the perceived value of their application. This how a professional basketball player comes to be worth $40 million a year.

Technical skills are very hard to come by and very valuable when you get them, especially if they have more content than general-purpose business programming. Six-figure incomes were not uncommon for consultants who "knew" a particular software product or a systems management methodology then in vogue. It is, therefore, a huge loss to the individual if–more probably when – individual skills become obsolete as when a new, better product comes along. Then an individual's marketability will quickly fade. He might even have to learn something completely new just to stay abreast.

This is when the cold, cruel logic of the market takes over: What if you are not as competent with a new product as you were with the old? Or what if you are late in learning the new product and you are now competing against younger, better qualified people? Then you might become one of those luckless has-beens, early to be laid off from your new career, eventually being left with some marginal job at a fraction of your previous salary. Just the possibility makes a person feel powerless and paper-thin. Technicians love solidity and control.

It was natural, therefore, that technical people would resist a business plan such as mine that would actually accelerate the obsolescence of their skills. I had seen technological insecurity all my working career and I expected staffs to resist the kind of change I proposed. In the first few years of my working life I knew a woman who resigned rather than switch from Autocoder – the IBM 1401 programming language – to Assembler – the base language for IBM 360 computers. This was why my business plan proposed that I would build my own separate business unit within an existing enterprise.

What I was not, however, prepared for was the antipathy with which salesmen and entrepreneurs both, supposedly the essence of risk-taking and open-mindedness, often greeted my proposals. And yet when I was actually confronted by their resistance or even the hint of it, it seemed logically consistent that they would. Consistent, that is, with the intangible factors that seemed to weigh against me: the linear, intuitive thinking of the managers, the resistance and even fear of change of the technicians, the perception that the business was what it was because of historical determinism, even the suggestion that IBM was less than an impervious monolith.

All of them fed at the trough of the insularity that had crept into the industry, just as the insularity fed off the human loathing of impermanence, the desire for unchangeable laws, the desire not to have to think, but just do. It was, I came to realize, as if I were asking to change the very foundation of their companies' culture.

Or, to put it another way, it was (I couldn't help but come up with this analogy) – as if the computer industry were an endless loop in which nothing outside the loop could ever penetrate because no exception can be allowed to occur. (In computerese a loop is a group of programmed instructions that performed over and over again – until something from the outside usually a programmer manually interrupting the program stops it.)

And, I thought to myself, how easy it must be, how comforting, to close yourself off from the outside universe this way. To never allow a different idea to challenge your self-constructed world. And how terrible it must be when a contradictory idea penetrates your consciousness anyway – and from such an unexpected source such as me.

I sensed that this might be the reason why, as I spun my story, I had the distinct feeling I was telling a four-year-old that there is no Santa Claus… as in the jiggling knee. It had happened during an interview with the vice-president of consulting of a large software firm.

As soon as I began to speak, his lips became pursed and his eyes lost their brilliance. Then he said, "Yes, well," and his conversation went on to other matters. And when I tried to come back to my pitch later on in our discussion, his face flushed. "But that's not what we're here to talk about. That's not the job we need." Even though my ideas were the way I had gotten in the door to begin with, it was as if he were constrained by rules he himself had set into place. Then he revealed the wonderful relationship he had with IBM and all the good things it had brought him and about the linear progress he saw for years ahead. As if there were no changes he anticipated beyond product improvements and no competition, either. All the time his knee was jiggling. And all this while scheduling a meeting for a formal presentation later.

And like the Madeline's in Marcel's tea in Proust's *In Search of Lost Time*, it was that image of the man's bouncing knee rippling his pin-stripe suit that has always brought back to me that time, and brought back the question I asked my wife the night I came back to Colony Square, "How could they dislike me so?"

It was an image that ran through my mind over and over again that night, a sleepless spring evening with the bedroom windows open and the sound of tires hydroplaning in the streets. It was an image from which all the millions of words that have poured out of my word processing software since...and the reason I am only now beginning to understand the pure complexity of it all. I had to understand why that image weighed on me.

When I at last gave up my dream and began to look for a *job*, as my mind had predicted so many years before, I was rejected over and over again for jobs I was sure I was best qualified for, I began to understand where all the time I had been trying to sell my ideas had led me.

I was going to sell myself as a consultant. Certainly, I had enough experience and pure brain power to be qualified to do that. And in my presenting my *bona fides* I could slip in some references to what I had learned about the computer business in its entirety.

I at last understood after one of those especially galling interview processes where you talk to a dozen or more people over weeks and weeks and everybody seemed enthusiastic about you and your abilities. Until the very end of the interviewing processing and you finally make your way back to the boss's office and you get to talking about real things. Then you sense it all slipping away and you can't do a thing about it, as if you were growing closer to a mirage in the desert. Then when you don't get the offer you expected and weeks go by and you've called the company a half-dozen times and finally, at last, you get one of those skinny envelopes in the mail with one of those kiss-off form letters...

I was so sure I had the job sewn up!

Why hadn't I? My tortured mind wouldn't let go of that thought. I must have reviewed the process a dozen times before that fateful day and night, but never so intensely. All I had ever come up with was the image of that damn jiggling knee from back when I was trying to build a business.

I began to understand why interviewing for a job was not all that different from selling an idea or a product. Even though I had abandoned my dream, I was still in a presentation mode. I was telling who I was rather than letting him find out for himself.

But this time I had the specter at Colony Square still fresh in my mind, after a long night and the days and weeks following just trying to bring some order to what I intuitively understood. I began to think of that interview, not just as a job lost, but in terms of a more general failure. Something fundamental had gone wrong between that man and me. Something that the jiggling knee suggested. Something that he had not been able to brush off. Some sign, the only one that had occurred to me in all those months, the only break in perception of what the industry was, what IBM was. Just this one little glimmer…Perhaps someone better suited to market a program like this, someone more impressive, more degrees perhaps, less interested in being understood, better known in the industry, would succeed where I had not.

I began to understand the impossibility of my being able to implement what I was proposing…and what my sense of personal failure actually amounted to.

My naivete going into this process had been monumental: my mistakes many. I had a vision, yes, an idea of some merit. It is still evident to me how powerful it might have been. Other people had made their way with much less.

Oh, yes, I understood the dynamics of the computer industry in a deep and subtle way. I had learned to read the surface personalities that people create for themselves and even predict how they would react in a given situation. But this was all too analytical, a bit distant, as if the person with which I was interviewing was a laboratory specimen I was dissecting.

And yet I am not insensitive–it is impossible to analyze the feelings of another without having had similar feelings one's self. Besides my techniques are more inductive than deductive. And so this interview, as had so many others, had failed because I did not connect with the man emotionally. How could this have happened?

Part of it was, as I have already said, because I *intentionally* went after his deepest needs. I didn't really like the man. During my life I had been betrayed so often that I trusted no one. I expected no one to understand me. And when I sensed the first sign of resistance, my suspicions were self-fulfilling prophecies. Rather than working to enlist him, I was contemptuous of him.

I was enjoying the feeling of being superior.

Was this the reason I chose to take the dilettantish intellectual tack in making my presentation? That I wanted him to know I was better than he was? Was this the reason I took on IBM when my ideas did not actually require him to understand the nature of the freight train heading full steam at him?

No, I told myself. I couched my interview the way I did because it was the only way I knew how to do it. As for IBM, I was only trying to gain credibility by revealing a truth they probably didn't know.

Sure, I was exasperated by my failure and rejection. Yet I really wanted to like the man and be liked in return. I had every reason to. Who can work for a man they don't respect?

And if I didn't like him after the interview, it wasn't out of some sour misanthropy, some embittered envy. It was my failure to make connection with him as a person. A failure of empathy that I sensed as soon as I walked out of his office, in fact while I was *in* his office. I wanted to grab him by the throat and tell him, "Pay attention to me. This is important." And the fact that I could not be so aggressive, that would have been unseemly, meant that I was doomed to never communicating to that impassive, unreceptive face...

For it was more than a company culture I was threatening, more even than an industry's view of itself, it was a view of reality itself.

Then what was this view? Why did he cling to it with such desperation when it was so clear – at some level to him as well as me that in doing so he risked his own creation?

At some level I understood – loyalty to existing staff, comfort with the company the way it was, a little ego, fear of the unknown; all factors that I have discussed before. At another level I was, however, still perplexed. What was the inner connection of all these strains? And what did that mean for the way business in general was organized? And my native land?

Why did it mean a repudiation of me? For it was me and not my ideas that didn't get the job.

Because — and this was a truly terrible realization — because my entire vision of reality was different from his. Yet it was his view of the truth, for all its irrationalities and inconsistencies, that was the norm, while mine was the aberration. I could afford to be completely rational, to be uninvolved with the conventional wisdom, because I was not a part of anything. In the deepest sense imaginable, I was an outlier everywhere.

But what was the world view implied by his seemingly scattered notions? For that matter, what was mine? In those answers lay the clue to my inability to be conventional.

I knew then that this would not be easy to find out. This man's perceptions and most of those like him had no articulated vision. To hope to understand what was happening to me, I would have to punch into another man's mind, into the deepest implications of a vision that was contrary to my own.

CHAPTER SEVENTEEN

MY LACK OF PAPER QUALIFICATIONS AND UNCONVENTIONAL MARKETING METHODS WORK AGAINST ME

This all felt true that dark night in 1988 and it feels even more true now. Yet at first my reason rejected the notion that the cause of my failure was something so metaphysical and intangible as a conflict in, of all things, world view. All my life I had learned to distrust a certain kind of self-examination, namely, the one that derives from a certain weakening and passive self-doubt. Goals are most often accomplished by going after them, to hell with the consequences. Even my prophetic streak, for all its source in my social insecurities, had always been directed to accomplishing some end.

What's more, the observations that form this book didn't come to my mind fully developed, all logical and worked out. Even the observations about IBM that formed the crux of my ideas, were in the beginning only partly formed concepts, intuition combined with bits and pieces of knowledge and experience. I wish I had I'd thought them through a little while longer, refined them a little more, but I was incapable of it then. As for the connection with my career, my ideas about how to properly start a consulting business were only random feelings at first, bits of thought, unconnected impressions. I had reason to be uncertain about them.

Perhaps, I thought, the reason I couldn't seem to get my message across lay not in my character but in technique. I was not, altogether introverted. Most people found me to be affable and sociable, a little hard to read perhaps, a bit of a loner, but on the whole a decent fellow. If my ideas were as good as I thought they were, there had to be somebody who would be receptive to them, Perhaps I wasn't getting to the right people.

The problem, I decided, must lie in my marketing system, a plausible enough conclusion to be sure. I had known all along that the best way to sell a concept like mine is to present it to a CEO as a business opportunity...and yet I had found it necessary to use the pretense of a job search as a way to get my foot in the door.

The reason I had selected such a back-stairs technique to promote myself was because I lacked the right kind of contacts. I had spent the best years of my working life as a middle manager and lacked the broad exposure of a career consultant or a salesman. An individual with no contacts has as little chance coming in from the cold as the Little Match Girl. Nor had I a long history of publications or advanced degrees.

Letters sent to CEOs wind up being filtered out by secretaries and junior executives. Telephone calls are rarely returned. Just showing up at a corporate office is a good way to talk to someone, provided that a receptionist doesn't leave you wedged on a couch all day. When you get to talk to some real official, too often the person you talk to is a functionary in personnel or a first line supervisor in the computer department.

But by presenting myself as a candidate for a job, there were plenty of people I could use as surrogates – executive search firms, former consulting associates, college chums – to get me to decision-makers. If a company was considering hiring someone who had my skills, there was at least an excuse to talk to the manager who did the hiring. Who knew what I could make of that opportunity?

Unfortunately for me, however, no executive begins the hiring process without having a very good idea of the kind of person, and often the specific catalogue of skills and education, he wants. The higher the position, the more rigid the implicit job description. Anyone that proposes an idea or has skills outside the template is immediately discounted.

The usual reason a company looks outside its ranks for a middle or senior manager is that there is a problem no one currently employed there can solve. Such a company is usually in serious trouble in at least one of its operations, since companies rarely deal with organizational problems until they become a crisis. Then management looks for a quick fix, one that such a program as I visualized would be unable to provide.

On the other hand, when the company is not in trouble, they sure as hell aren't going to invest a couple of hundred thousand dollars in somebody who is proposing to do something different from what the management thinks it needs.

This left me with two bad choices. If I tried to sell my prospective employer on the job I visualized, I would probably be rejected out of hand. If, on the other hand, I presented myself as a candidate for the job that was actually being offered, I might find myself locked into a set of duties nothing like the ones I hoped to do.

After many months of pushing myself as candidate for various positions, I realized that what I needed was not a job, but a company, preferably one that was currently successful; one that didn't think they had a problem managing their current enterprise. A business that was rich and stable enough to risk a change. Most important, one that was willing to take a chance on me.

I never found such a business, nor was I considered a serious candidate for all but a few of the jobs I sought, even after I decided not to sell my ideas until *after* I was employed. What's more the jobs I was offered were, I'm sure, in spite of my intellect rather than because of it. Most often, they were in sales.

I'm sure my employers thought that, properly channeled, my enthusiasm and promotional skills would make me a good representative of their company. I looked good in a business suit and was considered articulate and knowledgeable on many subjects. They hoped, I suspect, that I could be bought by a sizeable compensation package.

It turned out I was a mediocre bush-beating salesman. My lack of commitment to a company's products when all I wanted to do was to promote my own ideas invariably got in my way. I was, however, a very good closer.

Money was never my principal motivation, except, perhaps as a scorecard. I found the process of bush-beating and constant follow-up that is the normal sales process to be interesting only so long as I made a competitive game of it. Trouble is, that kind of game invariably comes down to lies and deception, false friendliness and contempt for your customers.

This is not to say that there aren't reputable salesmen in the software and services industry, but they are damn rare, and they became rarer still as the industry matured and sales grew harder to come by. I loathed myself for having to engage in it. As a means to escape the boredom and self-disgust, I would eventually revert to promoting my own ideas. But by that time I was typecast as a salesman and salesmen are not supposed to have ideas.

For one of the dark realities of modern life is that you are the role you play in your career. I was classified as a salesman and salesmen are supposed to be basic thinking people only interested in maximizing their income. Time spent structuring a business plan or preparing marketing materials was time I was not in the field pushing the company's products.

Inevitably this led to my employer and I becoming disenchanted with one another. I found myself drifting from job to unpromising job in disheartening succession. The more I moved from company to company, the more I exhausted the small capital of contacts I had built up. The periods between jobs grew longer and longer until there were no opportunities at all.

I suppose I would have been better off if I had spent more time learning the sales trade. If you are allowed only one talent in life, the most lucrative is the ability to recognize a business opportunity. This is the main reason a good salesman need never be out of a high-paying job. If I had been a little more salesy and a little less ethical, I might have found it easier to promote my ideas.

Had I, however, possessed all the promotional skills in the world, had I had the best organized presentation, I would still have found it difficult to sell myself as the kind of executive who could implement my vision.

oOo

I don't want you to think I was a total flop in finding a job that could lead to something. At Digital Equipment Corporation I was originally interviewed for a job running their demonstration center, but the powers that be decided they needed a salesman there instead of me. Eventually, I was hired as Software Consultant I, considered the second highest non-managerial rank in the software department. Even so, I took the job at a salary $3000 per year *less* than I made with the Big Eight firm I worked for previously.

It so happened that Ken Olsen, the CEO at Digital, realized that the minicomputer business had little future. Luckily, the company already had a sizeable services business, owing to all the high-quality technical people it had hired over the years. What Olsen thought he needed to do to save the company was to enter the projects business. He already had a senior services manager in the company headquarters near Boston so he was already planning to build a systems integration project organization from within. Surely, it was only a small jump from a rent-a-body business to a projects entity.

After several months grounding myself in company organization and procedures, I developed a business plan to sell my approach and I sent it to every senior manager in the company. I sold $25 million in business in one year, and was rewarded with a Software Excellence Award.

Then reality hit. I was assigned not to run the Projects business at the National level, nor at the Area level. Instead, I was promoted to a Software Services Consultant II to serve as a Management Consultant, one of two in the Area. Then, to build the Projects program, they hired a man who had been an internal project manager for a large company.

Now, managing a projects business as a consultant is altogether different from running one as an internal manager. Put the profit motive into a task and you have a far more disciplined set of constraints. For one thing it is the Project Manager himself who must be the front man to the customer not the Digital salesman. This is because it is his responsibility to estimate project duration and cost and present it to the customer. The account manager (salesman) may recognize an opportunity and be involved in the sales process, but cannot be the lead for that piece of work.

The best way to hunt for project-type opportunities is to assign a Management Consultant to do a preliminary study of as wide an area as she can manage and then cherry pick the best projects. For those projects the client has decided he wishes to pursue, a project manager is identified.

Both the Management Consultant and Project Manager must possess the same kind of personal attributes: leadership, personal presentation, ability to plan and control the project at many levels, etc. to win the confidence of client management as well as his own staff.

The internal project manager hired by Digital had none of these attributes. A couple of examples: He believed in regular staff meetings. Now, staff meetings are only effective if there is a well-planned topic or topics to be discussed. Otherwise, it wanders all over the place. To avoid this pitfall the manager of a staff meeting (not necessarily the manager of a function) must know exactly the topics to be discussed and how much time it will take to discuss it. If any topic runs over, the staff meeting manager must find a convenient stopping point and reschedule the discussion. As you might guess, this means staff meetings can only work with an internal organization. If you try to force staff meetings over a field organization, you are pulling people out of the field for at least two days (one to organize a presentation, the other to get to the main office and make the presentation), days that ought to be in the field doing work, days that ought to be chargeable.

If you are not careful, the staff meeting might be scheduled at a time inconvenient for at least some of the participants. Early on in his tenure, the ex-internal project manager ordered me to attend a staff meeting rather than participate in a multi-million-dollar sales call. The sales manager of the account went over his head to protest. Needless to say, I went to the sales call, in spite of my manager's threats and cajolery.

He continued to push the staff meetings idea even when it was evident to all that it was getting in the way of project sales and performance.

What he should have done was to schedule a once a quarter gathering of *all* the staff in which each project manager formally presented his work progress and classes were taught on the various project management techniques and other necessary skills. Such a meeting would be scheduled well in advance and occupy at least three days.

The ex-internal project manager was sarcastically nicknamed "Staff Meetings" by his subordinates.

Then it came time for my annual salary increase. After all my accomplishments, I received a paltry $1,500 a year increase, still less than I was making as a Big Eight consultant. I'm sure this travesty was caused by the fact that pay was budgeted at the beginning of the year and awarded at mid-year, which meant six months of accomplishments were ignored.

When my new pay rate was revealed to me, the ex-internal project manager apologized and told me I could get more if I appealed. If you think it's wrong, I thought to myself, you should have fixed it before you came to me. I'm sure it was another instance of a silly bureaucratic rule that the man psychologically couldn't work around. He was too wedded to rules and procedures.

Then, when the company hired a second management consultant, they hired an independent, classified her as a Software

Consultant III and paid her significantly more than me. She had no experience with consulting methodologies, became frustrated with all the rules and soon left the company.

Desperate, I also left the company for a very shaky entrepreneurial venture marketing parallel supercomputers. Biggest mistake of my life.

oOo

I had one more opportunity to show my stuff as an inventor of a project management business. Integral Systems Incorporated was a software company that had once upon a time dominated the Personnel/Payroll systems business, but was facing tough competition from Peoplesoft, later to become the gold standard in Payroll/Personnel. To expand its product line, Integral had recently acquired a middle-of-the-road accounting suite.

Integral had a small staff of people that had experience with their systems and assisted customers with the implementation process. Unfortunately, Integral had given away the much larger systems integration business to third parties, some of which had developed enhancements to the base system. Technically, these companies were illegal (as was Peoplesoft), since they used program code developed at Integral. As was the case in most companies of the era, all employees at Integral had signed a waiver giving the company the rights to any work products developed while employed there. Integral never pursued any legal action against its former employees however.

Which is where I came in. By then Integral needed to pursue any profitable business it could lay its hands on, including software development projects. Since many businesses wanted to look to a single vendor to assume responsibility for a successful implementation, Integral had the inside track to any such project. My ideas were an exact fit for such a business.

Unfortunately, there were a number of internal managers who also aspired to run such a business and believed their product knowledge was enough. During my first weeks there, I developed a detailed business plan for how I would approach the implementation market. This immediately stimulated jealousy and resentment.

Early on at Integral I participated in a project for the State of Maryland where IBM was the prime contractor. Maryland had written detailed specifications as to what they wanted the software to do, much of which was not available in the Integral product. Maryland wanted a line item estimate for each function they had described. I was informed by Integral that there was a young woman in the Toronto office who had developed a foolproof estimation tool.

I forwarded the state's specifications to Toronto only to receive back a single figure. It seems her wonderful estimation tool depended solely on the number of employees in the company or institution. This might have worked for a relatively small company where Integral would be assigning employees to train the staff and perform a few enhancements. For the State of Maryland one figure was completely unresponsive.

Company management insisted that I use the figure given me. Instead, I gauged the relative size of each enhancement and came up with a point scale for each. Then I aggregated the points and developed a ratio for each enhancement. I multiplied these ratios by her original cost estimate and came up with a figure for each enhancement and included these estimates in the line item proposal. The process infuriated her and her many supporters in the company,

This, along with several other impossible-to-manage events at Integral led to my being let go in a little over a year.

If you add these experiences and a couple of others to the outright rejections I received, you can appreciate how my battle with internal cultures led to the end of my career.

oOo

Yet there were other factors that led me down the garden path. It was not because my plan was not well thought out or I wasn't impressive enough personally, but because my resume wasn't nearly so strong as my aspirations required.

Intuitively, I had always understood my resume would be a stumbling block, yet analytically this made no sense to me. Because I had spent my career concentrating on accomplishments rather than pushing my way up the ladder, I had never achieved a status equal to my talents. Did this mean I was weaker, less competent than those who had gone the other way? Quite the reverse.

Why should a resume make so much of a difference, anyway? Why wouldn't the quality of a person's ideas, his skill in presenting them, his references, his list of accomplishments mean more than a few fancy-looking titles on a sheet of watermarked vellum?

For two reasons, I discovered. First, we are becoming an abstracted, systematized civilization and the resume is the grease that makes "human resources" work. Secondly, because people are expected to embellish, exaggerate, hell, even lie on a resume. If a man's documentation looks worse than his interview would lead you to believe, the human reality behind the document is likely to be worse still.

Now imagine what would happen when I presented my resume, even supposing I managed to reach the right person and had convinced him that I knew what I was talking about? Suppose I generated a huge amount of enthusiasm as to my ideas and the executive and I were exactly simpatico.

And then he looked more closely at my resume. That would stop him cold, wouldn't it?

For all my claims to career accomplishments, for all the projects completed and innovations implemented, for all the creativity and track record of personal and technical leadership, I had never held a position higher than Systems and Programming Manager in a Fortune 600 company. In the years since that job I had other major accomplishments, but mostly I had been thrashing around career-wise with little to show for my efforts but scars.

Now what would you think should you be hiring an executive and saw such a resume? It would give you pause, wouldn't it? And would it help or hurt that I seemed conventional, conservative, organized, intelligent? Especially when, time after time, right on the cusp of success, something happened that led to my being fired or resigning?

And now you present a whole raft of ideas that fly in the face of conventional wisdom.

Is there something self-destructive going on? You'd ask yourself. Or some disqualifying weakness in personality. Maybe an inability to play well with others.

If I were as powerful and competent as I believed, my interviewer would ask himself, why would I settle for a job now when I could just as easily build my own company where the opportunity to create real wealth is so much the greater? Oh, he could understand why I might be too willful to make it in some corporate bureaucracy. I might irritate my superiors when I tried to present some absurd notion. If they hired me, they might want to advance someone less contentious instead of me; they might want to fire me.

Why then *didn't* I make my own way. Wouldn't that prove my contention? Did my excuse that I needed a critical mass of people to get started hold water.

Then there was my message, so radical, so challenging, so counterintuitive. Could it be trusted when it seemed so equivocal, so opposed to the ideas that had proven true since the founding of the computer industry.

What if I had toned it down a bit, made it a little less threatening? What if I appealed a little more to the needs and prejudices of my prospects? What if appeared more down-to-earth, more of a regular guy?

Probably more hopeless sales jobs.

I knew that too much change in personality was impossible. The more I donned the guise of the back-slapping country club type, the more unconventional I would seem.

oOo

Given that perspective, I suppose it is remarkable that anyone would have taken a chance on me. Yet I did have a couple of opportunities to make something out of myself.

It's no wonder that years later, when IBM's struggles *did* translate into much slower growth for the firms that leached off their technology, that the executives of these businesses inevitably hired a Partner from some large management consulting firm or a senior manager from a competitor to do what I was sure I could do better.

It all came down to *risk*. Rather than the radical insight I offered, a Partner would provide structure to the conventional answers. Incremental rather than more significant change. And while it might never have the pure glossy panache a business run my way would possess, incrementalism would succeed …for a while at least. And, most importantly, such an executive could buy time to make mistakes and recover from them, because no one would question a Partner's competence or track record.

Unfortunately, few of these companies took advantage of their time or make changes beyond the first couple of steps and would eventually fail. And in the longer view the Partner's conventional wisdom would not result in the necessary rethinking of the entire process that the dynamics of the industry demanded. And if their clients didn't recognize that they were lost.

By the time the industry shakeout had gotten cranked up, it was 1992, and industry executives were scurrying around looking for answers and experimenting with change…though not from me. Being right too early invariably leads to rejection later, because that would mean admitting I was smarter than industry executives were. After a dozen rejections and some failures when I was thwarted making the necessary alterations to current practice, I was no longer credible even as the project manager I had been twenty-five years before. I was now fifty years old, an age when if you are out a job, it is assumed you are dead wood. I would have been a fool not to be discouraged then.

I suppose I was numb to it …or perhaps I had already begun to set my life in a different trajectory. By 1992 it all seemed such an old story. I had known my business career was a terminal case since that terrible night four years before. All those years in between I had been merely playing out the string…out of pride or lack of any alternative, I suppose.

CHAPTER EIGHTEEN

THE CONCLUSION TO MY BUSINESS CAREER

The gradual discovery of the consequences of my inability to sell my ideas led me to many sleepless nights. And when the full force of my realization hit me weeks after, I sat up straight in bed. I stared into the dark, my t-shirt soaked from the sweat of my anxiety. Yes, I tried to tell myself, my mistakes were correctable. But what mistakes! What corrections! Was I up to it.

Yet people with far less ability had bulled their way into success. Why not me? A bad resume was not necessarily a disqualification. While it was true that my marketing methods had been flawed, were they *that* self-destructive? One can always find fault with their own methods. Look too hard…therein lies paranoia. Self-criticism is often the most disabling of traits…

But there was something else…

Trust your feeling, I told myself, not your reason alone. There was something not right about me…

But what?

Realizing that sleep once more was a lost cause, I turned on the bedside lamp. My wife winced awake and rolled over, burying her head between her pillows. Guiltily, I turned the lamp off. But I was too anxious for sleep. "What is it?" my wife mumbled from deep inside the covers.

And so, when as I often do when I am in one of my night moods, I got out of bed, went downstairs to the living room and settled into the armchair underneath the bookcase beside the fireplace. I reached for one of the many volumes of the Eleventh Edition of the Encyclopedia Britannica, opened its crumbling cover and inattentively perused the article on Botany while my mind raced.

I was confused, my mind a tangled thicket of conflicting impulses. Nothing made sense.

All right, I told myself, I had gone after a job to manage big projects and had been reduced to being a "rent-a-programmer" salesman. Well, there had been misapprehensions on both sides.

You're allowed a mistake once in a while. Yes, I'll admit I had gone way beyond my capabilities this time, into something I was totally ill-equipped to do. I had been arrogant – no, beyond arrogant irresponsible, since I had to make a living somehow – in pursuing an impossible dream so late in my career.

But why should I beat myself up for being arrogant, since it is only by going beyond mere self-esteem is anything accomplished. Better by far to have tried and failed then to settle for the mediocrity into which the world seemed to pigeon-hole me. If I couldn't make a career out of my insights, for whatever reason, I had other options albeit most of them were pretty ordinary.

I had better get on with it, though. Time was running short.

oOo

Or so I reasoned. I sensed there was something other than reason working on me, however. Something which had goaded me into this unlikely and ultimately self-destructive path and kept me after it long beyond my realization that all was lost. I am not by nature aggressive or all that arrogant, not that self-confident even. What self-confidence I have is fragile, easily driven into fear. And here I'd been seized by this compelling urge to make a big splash, followed ultimately by a feeling of abject and inexcusable failure. Nothing seemed to be able to stop me. What did all this mean?

I mulled over that question for most of the remaining hours of darkness. I racked my brain without satisfactory resolution until before dawn when I finally fell asleep, still sitting in the armchair. The Encyclopedia Britannica was still open to the unread article.

I awoke to the bright mid-morning sunlight streaming through the French doors. My wife had already left for work. It seemed I had found the answer.

My entire life had been wrong – at first it was as vague as this – its direction, all the various career decisions I had made, the very way I had approached my work. All wrong.

It's true I had gone through a lot in the years before my insight and its pursuit. My mother's death, a long and harrowing divorce, a transfer to a city where I knew nobody, being forced out of a job I was uniquely qualified to perform, an entirely new career I wasn't at all sure I could master.

Yet the quality of my current marriage was better than I had reason to hope and my health was good. I even had new friends that seemed to like me. I had reason to be proud of who I was. I had survived shocks that would have crushed another person.

In spite of my current feelings about things, there wasn't anything wrong with my character. I was not weak or incapable. My ethics were of the highest order. Too high, in truth; I would not lie or cheat just to get ahead. Others would. Life had failed me, not the other way around.

Yet I could not entirely escape the responsibility for what had happened to me. For all those years of working twice as hard as my peers, with twice the concentration, and many accomplishments. For all my appearance of sociability and willingness to (falsely) conform, I had come to this place in my life because I wanted to be affirmed, not by an image I showed the world, but me as I really was. I would not be classified.

If a person is not classified, however, then what are they? A misfit is the label they give you and a misfit is the last label you want affixed to you.

I had known this from the time I wore sailor suits. Then why did I pursue this lonely, misunderstood course?

There is the matter that I was right about IBM and the course of the industry, and about the way consulting ought to be done.

But there are also the consequences of being classified. When you are classified, you lose your right to be something else. You can never change, although the human spirit is never static and never just one thing. To try to make yourself be the classification you are assigned, you can never locate the real, authentic self.

Of course, you can be one thing on the surface and quite another in your marrow. I had done that most of my life. But if you have any self-knowledge, you know that's what you're doing, don't you? And doesn't that knowledge make you take something off the pitch? I know it did me.

Most successful people I knew (success being define as much by achievement as much as rank and salary) seemed to lie easy with who they presented themselves to be. Why couldn't I?

There must, I concluded, be something essential in my makeup that was different from my fellows, something neither effort nor talent could overcome, a fundamental rhythm that was in conflict with the way the world worked. That must be the source of my personal crisis!

oOo

If that were true, however, then my epiphany could not have been a once in a lifetime experience. Life has a way of repeatedly exploiting weak links no matter how much we try to protect ourselves from its shocks. This is why our unhappy experiences are invariably repeated.

Several times in the past a kind of mad anxiety had absorbed me. It always came as an emotional understanding of sufficient force that it penetrated the analytical veneer I clutched onto, a frenzy as if driven on by a subliminal need, a sense of something intolerably wrong.

The first time I had experienced this kind of psychic pain was when I was a Sophomore at the Virginia Military Institute. A new administration had changed the character of the corps of cadets so that it would become more abstractly military and less personally brutal. Hazing and the class system were deemphasized; hierarchy and military discipline were substituted. On the surface this was more systematic and more like the real Army, but it was brought about by a group of career officers who were just itching to test their leadership theories in combat. Most cadets had signed on assuming they would serve in the peacetime Army. While I was too young to verbalize my intuition, it led me to make a foolish gesture that wound up forcing me out of school. Only years later would the shambles that was the Vietnam War make my discomfort tangible.

I had also experienced this same sort of fear-borne anxiety near the end of my careers at A.H.Robins and Digital and at the time of my divorce. Each time there was a cause for my reaction that I could sense but not explain.

Each time I was alone in my feeling. When I expressed it to my peers, they looked at me as if I had gone mad. That such an ordinarily calm fellow, even a bit passive, was now such a wild-eyed enthusiast for such an unpromising idea. What a big fuss about nothing!

But this was different. I had not gone into this phase of my life without understanding the possible consequences. I had a backup plan if it didn't work out the way I expected it to. I had always recovered from the disasters of life before. Some people referred to me as a survivor.

But now I was defeated in an existential sense. There would be no coming back. My computer industry career was over. What was coming would be radically different from what had passed. I had completely drained my competitive resources.

I had failed to convince anybody that I was worth a job commensurate with my accomplishments. I could no longer bear trying. I was ashamed of where I was; I tried to suppress it; I denied it. But as this whole book has shown, once you have grown to understand a truth, self-denial will always fail.

oOo

This difficulty in making myself understood, I have since learned, is the penalty you pay when you search for meaning and the world around is trying to build things. When you are deconstructing the symbolic content of social culture, you will not be understood and you will probably be resented.

And you will never know if the meaning you have discovered has any real utility. When you ask not *how* to accomplish an end but *why* accomplish it at all, you won't always be drawn to a standard process. If you ask yourself why do it the way it has always been done, you open yourself to a kind of speculation which may lead nowhere and produce little. Furthermore, you have nothing and nobody else to justify yourself – no precedent, no authority–when you *are* able to discover some new ideas. Nothing but your own conscience, and you can never really be sure that's not flawed, too.

It's a lot easier to succumb to the status that life affords you, to be practical and ordinary. It's what I had tried to do all my life with some success, too. Not that I particularly liked doing it: only those tangible successes had given me the energy to keep at it. To fail and be inauthentic at the same time; that was intolerable!

But what if failure isn't failure at all (is any outcome that arises from desire ever failure)? And what if success seems like failure when measured by the conventional yardstick. What if making a system work or, for that matter, building a business empire, was not true to the authentic me? What if my purpose was only to understand and communicate?

oOo

How was I to do that? Ah, that was a sticky question. If there are rhythms in a person's character which are not reducible to analysis and correction. If, in fact, character exists and is not an infinitely malleable hash of possibility, then I would have to go beyond the analytical, beyond my prophetic gifts, which, after all, are only a measure of surface personality, a *persona*, if you will. I would have to find a new way to understand my demons.

And how was I to find that way? What means did I have to translate a vague sensibility into something that is not just understood but organized and communicated? How does one approach which seems to be ineffable?

The answer lay in writing it down, but not in the conventional narrative but by probing into as deep a meaning as you can. Not to allow yourself to abandon the ship before it fairly sails, but to keep haggling after your insights until you are satisfied you have it. Which is what this book attempts to do.

CHAPTER NINETEEN

WHAT HAPPENED NEXT

Most disastrous for IBM was the development of PC "clones" which were sold at a lower price than IBM's product, needing to pay for its massive overhead, could. A computer clone was a Personal Computer which functioned exactly like an IBM PC. This was made possible by the fact that the IBM PC had only one part that was proprietary to IBM. If a company could "reverse engineer" that part and design one that was similar but not exactly the same, they could build an IBM type computer themselves.

IBM had bought its internals from Intel and operating system from Microsoft. Both were more than willing to sell their proprietary technology to a third-party manufacturer. Although the cost of developing these technologies became large, the size of the market was in the millions. If you could develop and manufacture a chip for a million dollars and sell three million copies at a $1 each you could make a fortune.

These were economies that a number of companies found attractive especially if they could hold down their fixed costs. The first company to understand this was Compaq. Once Compaq had product availability, it almost immediately grabbed a huge share of the market. Others followed. Building a Personal Computer became so easy that mom-and-pop local computer jocks were making them. My first PC was built this way.

Of course, computer hobbyists had been building all or part of computers for years. Altair, TRS-80s, were just a couple of examples. But they offered no support or software. CP/M, the early operating system, was available, but any application for which you used it had to be programmed in machine language, which was no easier to master than Finnish. These hobbyist computers were notoriously underpowered. Only dedicated computer people were willing to engage in building such a beast from scratch.

Apple was another matter. Many pundits believe that the IBM was the first commercial PC. It wasn't. Apple had developed a complete system where everything was proprietary and emphasized user friendliness a couple of years before IBM. It is my conviction that it was the Apple competition that pressured IBM into developing its own computer so quickly.

Apple lost out in the first round because IBM developed its own portfolio of applications software. Moreover, it had the IBM name on its machines. In the early 1980s the IBM cachet was at its peak. Third parties rushed to develop software for IBM machines. Spread sheets proliferated, as did word processing software. Although early PCs featured near-letter-quality dot matrix printers, which used pin feed continuous forms, and were useless for formal correspondence, they were plenty good enough for ordinary documents and reports.

Apple competed by developing an icon-driven user interface which made it much easier to initiate an application than the first-generation "slash and special character commands". But Microsoft quickly developed a competing product of its own. They called it Windows. The entire package soon became known as the IBM PC, and dominated the PC business. During these tough years Apple stayed in the game, however, much like the Seven Dwarfs of the early mainframe era.

IBM's inability to compete or maintain its traditional profit margin in what had become a commodity business led it to eventually sell off its Personal Computer business. Even today, however, the original IBM standard using Microsoft and mainly Intel parts is the big boy in the industry.

Big Blue was, however, eventually able to circumvent the mainframe's limitations by its introduction of Advanced Peer-to-Peer Computing under which PCs were able to communicate directly to each other. This was many years after such a capability was generally available on other companies' machines. On balance IBM could not retain its revenue stream or profitability selling computers alone.

Since PCs were sold at an increasingly low price that many could afford, they became a rapidly growing industry. Until the development of the Internet, however, it was still a relatively small and low profit business, no competition with mainframes, except as intelligent terminals replacing dumb ones. Used this way, PCs still had to be hooked up to a mainframe.

I was right about one thing. A few years later after my initial prophecy, IBM went into a decline that resulted in its no longer being the dominant force in the industry, only a big player. Mainframe technology was not the *dernier cri* any more. The years of struggle the company spent trying to make do with the old IBM rules led it nowhere but to further decline.

The development of server systems that used the power of the microchip to collect data from many clients to do what were usually specialized processing (like quickly locating data on massive disk farms or follow pathways to subordinate processors).

Eventually, IBM was forced to hire the first CEO who did not grow up through the IBM system, Lewis Gerstner. Gerstner changed the company into one that emphasized software and services rather than "big iron." This seemed to be in conflict with the antitrust agreement of the 1970s, but by this time the company was far from being the near monopoly of its glory days, and the government let the apparent conflict go.

Not that Big Blue abandoned the hardware business entirely. There were too many customers wedded to its brand of business computing for that to happen. Also, mainframe computing remained very profitable. Still, it lost market share in the larger computer industry both in absolute and relative terms.

I was wrong about the technologies that would replace it, however. I believed that minicomputers would become the intermediate systems between desktop terminals and the central computer. After all, minicomputers were the basis for networking and word processing systems in that era. In the mid-1980s Personal Computers were comparatively expensive per unit of power and didn't compete well with minicomputer-based systems.

But minicomputers turned out to be an interim technology. Personal Computers became much more powerful and provided much more capacity in both internal and auxiliary (disk) memory. But this took a while to materialize.

In the meantime, IBM, Digital and others formed a consortium to develop a new generation of microchip, much more powerful than existing microprocessors. Their goal was to grab back their share of the computer industry and shut out the emerging PC competition.

Sadly for IBM, the stagnation in microchip power was only a temporary aberration. Soon Moore's Law took over and the PC processor of today was as powerful as the mainframe of a year or two before. Furthermore, IBM lacked control over the chip fabrication business. Intel did. Eventually, IBM gave up on the microchip market.

Companies that once would have been mainframe customers now went with server farms as their central system. I'm sure you have seen videos of massive server racks lined up row after row seeming to stretch to infinity. Client-server technology was especially useful to the emerging internet-based companies, since they had no legacy systems to replace.

Even the services business Lewis Gerstner had banked on had limitations. There were many very large companies offering the same kind of services with very long histories of accomplishment. These companies had all the infrastructure, methodologies, contacts, big names in the industry, and highly skilled specialists, that IBM initially lacked. The absolute size of the software and services business was huge, but remained fragmented. Since this was an entirely new business for it, IBM's overall revenue increased while its mainframe business remained static.

IBM was, however, limited as to how far it could stretch the software and services market. Recently, IBM had fourteen consecutive quarters of declining revenues.

It is now banking on super high technology systems to bring them back, the kind that requires university-style research capabilities, the kind that IBM had never been particularly good at. The big two at the moment are Artificial Intelligence (which is a bit of a misnomer since it covers a large number of sins, most of which are not truly intelligent in the way human beings are) and massively parallel supercomputer systems, which, as we have seen, are only useful for certain scientific applications, many of which take years to develop.

oOo

Then came the Internet and the World Wide Web (WWW). I saw the beginning of this technology in 1965, when I worked at the Defense Personnel Support Center in Philadelphia. Widespread networks were being used to expedite the supply chain using the Defense Department's Autodin,

Many years later private concerns had tapped into the much higher capacity fiber optics allowing a totally interconnected World Wide Web. Such companies as AOL became the switching hubs, called Internet Service Providers (ISPs). Personal Computers were now able to communicate directly to one another across local, regional and national boundaries at high speeds and without the interference of governments (mostly) and large corporations. ISPs consisted of banks of server systems and really massive disk farms enhanced by so-called "Cloud Computing". Organizations could now build web sites where their customers could communicate with them from anywhere in the country and do business with them directly without need for brick and mortar stores.

Since large retailers were slow to grasp the implications of this radically new business model, startup businesses such as Amazon.

com were the first to take advantage of the Internet. In the 1980s and 1990s internet businesses proliferated like kudzu. Probably 90% had an extremely poor business idea or, in some cases, virtually none at all. But they all could raise a significant amount of money from Venture Capitalists (VCs). VCs had been showering money on computer industry companies since the beginning, but most of their early investments had gone to hardware makers or business software developers.

Since the internet had already been built, hardware was not really a factor in such businesses. Almost all internet companies are based on program code alone. I have frequently told people who were enamored of some new piece of equipment, "Forget Intel, the real profitability in the business lies with Microsoft." Although developing a new piece of equipment is usually capital-intensive, highly risky and must be completely viable the day it goes to market, entry into the software industry requires little or no capital investment. It can be brought to fruition in as little as a couple of months with one or a few programmers and will continue to expand so long as there are coders available and ideas to support them.

I also predicted the bursting of the Internet bubble around the turn of the millennium. I couldn't see how the irrational enthusiasm for any new idea could sustain itself. It smelled of Tulipomania or the South Sea Bubble. Two weeks before the sudden collapse of the boom, I was watching television when some brilliant Asian guru said about the industry, "it makes all kinds of sense." And proceeded to regurgitate an incomprehensible spiel as to why he thought so. It's my experience that all practical ideas must be easy to explain, incremental and not radical, and obey its own logic, not some general theory. What he was telling us was way too academic and pure madness.

In spite of the collapse of the internet bubble, a number of web-based companies managed to survive. Gradually as more and more people began to understand the power of the Internet, many, if not most, retail customers turned away from brick and mortar stores to online purchasing, until giant shopping malls became ghost towns. And many famous retailers fell by the wayside or saw their business shrink. Even the Macy's Thanksgiving Day parade, not to speak of Macy's itself, seems set for the chopping block.

Apple did come back…by rehiring Steve Jobs as CEO. Jobs understood that there was a market for pricy, high-quality and innovative computers. With IBM no longer in the PC game, Apple had no famous name to compete against. Further, Apple introduced a number of computer-based products that expanded their product line exponentially, Ipad, Iphone, etc. Their control over software vendors resembled IBM's in the mainframe era.

Notice that all of these products, indeed those in the entire PC industry made the computer a consumer product. Which meant the number of potential customers for any new platform were astronomical. It was no longer unusual for a household to have two, three, or more computers tied into the Internet.

Beginning in the 1980s microchips began to be found in a number of electromechanical devices, vacuum cleaners, smart phones, stoves, etc. Soon robots performed a number of processes in the automobile and aircraft assembly businesses. Practically no discrete product manufacturing company operated without computers managing some part of the process. Automobiles and airplanes had computers aboard to monitor the equipment and allow for new technologies such as Global Positioning System (GPS) to track the car's current position and map out a destination. Soon driverless cars will become feasible for the mass market.

In none of these technologies did you see the name IBM. Big Blue was not the sort of business that successfully marketed bits and pieces. Even had IBM maintained its traditional revenue stream, its market share was bound to shrink.

The second watershed in computing was the transfer of the main source of wealth from hardware to software. Virtually, all the giant new companies in the industry are software-based and do not require the invention of any new equipment. Yahoo, Google, Facebook, Linkedin and all the other social network companies. Almost all these enterprises were developed independently from IBM by "tech geeks" who were far away from the IBM paradigm.

Computers also penetrated the Executive Suite. In the early days IBM had intentionally kept senior management ignorant of their own computer applications. Most senior managers saw computers as a machine divorced from the intellectual work they performed. You never saw a middle manager with a typewriter did you? This began to change as dumb terminals became visible in most back-office systems. It took, however, the introduction of the Personal Computer to change everything.

Corporate Executives now had computers on their desk. It was easier to send an e-mail than to try to schedule a meeting with a subordinate or peer or pass on information. Some managers found it easier to do their own spreadsheets than to delegate them to a clerk who might be incapable of managing something that complex.

All of a sudden CEOS were computer literate. Unfortunately, they were rarely literate about the applications development process and the bet-the-business assets and liabilities of using computer technology. The communications gap between computer and functional management persisted. Frequently, what seemed easy to a CEO was very difficult to implement in an existing computer program. This led even famously people-oriented companies to go through several management regimes in a half-dozen years.

In none of these games was IBM able to play. It's true they were able to create a pretty good server system, but the profitability of such devices, even if you sold a lot of them, was nowhere near the aggregate profitability of their mainframe and small business computer lines. In none of the emerging technologies could IBM's culture and computer design function as well as those of the emerging technology companies.

As to the services business: while IBM had an advantage in its name and the business was extremely profitable, the project management market was very crowded and competition was stiff. Besides, IBM did not understand the consulting business and failed to win contracts by attempting to use salesmen to market them and generalists to man them. Although no one tried to build a business with the sophistication of my proposal, several firms used parts of it, such as having management and staff dedicated to a particular application or business department. The industry had, however, become highly fragmented in the skills required. With more than one computer, you needed specialists in hardware, network design, capacity planning, perhaps an Artificial Intelligence specialist, another for data mining, etc.

Soon enough IBM became a bit player in business services. And their applications software was always inferior to that of the independent vendors. Although it gained much notoriety in the supercomputer industry, parallel supercomputers remained difficult to program.

IBM is no longer the most valuable company in its own industry. Apple, Amazon.com, Google, etc. exceed IBM by far.

This was the time of the close of my career. If you read between the lines you already know that in spite of the fact that I had sold against IBM for years I had grown up with IBM technology and was an IBM type through and through.

One of my assets in the mainframe era was that I was tall, lean, and not unattractive and wore a business suit well. I could write well enough to have considered a literary career when I was young. When I became a Management Consultant, I polished my presentation skills and could communicate an idea with the best of them. Along with my strong technical background, I became a very competent consultant. I could also close with the best of them since by the time the deal was near closure, I knew the client well enough to craft a presentation, often littered with literary quotations, that gave him confidence that I could do the work.

Although my surface presentation was professional, my authentic core was very unconventional. I was an autodidact with a prodigious memory. And I had both intuitive and analytical thinking processes. I could see both the big picture and the components that made it up.

I found early on that my personality and intellectual skills were not always an advantage, often threatening, and I intentionally toned them down in job interview or a proposal. It is not for nothing that virtually every job has a job description, limiting its scope and detailing in great specificity the experience and educational requirements. My capabilities were much broader than that, but I hid those that seemed irrelevant.

Even when I was an internal computer manager at AH Robins, I had very special skills. Although I was never a programmer, I nevertheless learned the functions and organization of each of the thousands of programs for which I was responsible. This made it easy for me to figure out what had gone wrong and how to fix it. I could quickly determine how new applications might best fit into the overall scheme of things.

But it took a while to figure all this out for any new company with which I might consult. It was also a liability in implementing a software package, which, it turned out was often more difficult than to build an application from scratch. Thus, the work I did as a management consultant I found tedious and unnecessarily time consuming. It was out of desperation that I looked for other opportunities and formed my plan.

When I finally gave up that phase, I discovered I was in a wholly different world than the one had left.

It had long been known that programmers were cut from a different cloth than other business people. They were comfortable working alone and turning the abstract into the concrete. They refused to conform to business norms in dress and manners. Their social skills were barely adequate. Although they were paid well to begin with, they were often regarded as little more than clerks. Many cared more about their technical specialty than the business as a whole. Advancement outside the programmer ranks within the computer department was rare and next to impossible in other areas of their organization.

All my career I had avoided programming, mainly because I cared more about the larger business problem and how computerization might make it work more effectively. Now, I found that without coding skills nobody perceived they needed me.

This is because job requirements in the field were far different than in the past. No longer could a person qualify for a computer position without at least an associate's degree in computer science or business automation. Virtually all managers and systems analysts came up through the ranks. Project development was now performed in groups where everybody had a say in design, target dates for their own work, and even organizational structure.

Later, a position was formed in many companies that I had pushed for in the 1980s, namely, a "computer czar", or more formally, a Chief Information officer (CIO), who was responsible for all computerization in a business and was often on the level of the CFO or the senior vice president of sales and marketing.. This position was recognition of the growing importance of the computer in a company's operations.

I felt I was uniquely qualified for such a position, but no one would consider me for it anymore after a nearly ten-year hiatus. Actually, I had in the 1980s tried to sell the idea through my consulting assignments.

In the industry as a whole, programming skills came to dominate. PC applications were often created by programmers and its creators could sometimes become billionaires overnight. Specialists in certain software products or in emerging technologies such as network design, data mining and artificial intelligence could form large companies or charge exorbitant hourly rates.

There was no longer a place for my skills.

Since I was only in my fifties, I had to find a place to work elsewhere. Since I was regarded as a promising literary maven in college and before, I thought I would build a literary career. After a mixed reception in several writer's conferences, I matriculated in the Master of Fine Arts in Fiction Writing program at Georgia State University. After a discouraging experience writing stories and a couple of novels for (no) publication, I gave that up. I had spent too many years writing proposals, specifications, training manuals and the like to think like a story-teller

Next, I decided to try Social Work. On the day before my sixty-fifth birthday I received my MSW (Masters in Social Work). The social work job I then took in a Hospice company was a disaster for me, since I was unwilling to compromise my ethics. Later on, I used my social work skills by building a local program for the National Alliance on Mental Illness (NAMI). Once more I was extremely successful, but at the end of a year-and-a-half, I discovered that there was no one willing to join me in selling the program.

Several years before I received a large sum of money from my father's estate and more in a divorce settlement. I was set for life.

And this is when I quit entirely.

Except for writing two non-fiction books, this being one of them.

www.ingramcontent.com/pod-product-compliance
Ingram Content Group UK Ltd.
Pitfield, Milton Keynes, MK11 3LW, UK
UKHW022228230426
12048UKWH00016BA/1130